Intelligence

Corporate Success and Vigilance

Attention Authors

Manas Publications is fighting a war to tell the world that India can win the battle not only by bullet but also by pen. We are converting fighters into writers since our country is full of intellectuals but their knowledge is only confined to them. No sincere effort has been made by any publisher to give the right direction to their knowledge and the talent of intellectual is still hidden. An author always gives the raw material in the shape of manuscript and it is the sense of publisher to make it a finished product. We are motivating the intellectuals' mind and publishing their manuscripts for more than two decades and would like to publish your manuscript too. If you or your colleagues have any manuscript or are working on, please don't hesitate to contact us with detailed synopsis and contents for its publication. We take utmost care in production and give a wide publicity to the book and its author. We can also suggest you the title for writing related to your subject, since we are the publishers who believe more in quality than in quantity.

Intelligence

Corporate Success and Vigilance

D.C. Pathak, IPS

Former Director : Intelligence Bureau

Manas Publications

New Delhi-110002 (INDIA)

MANAS PUBLICATIONS
(Publishers, Distributors, Importers & Exporters)
4402/5-A, Main Ansari Road
(Opp. HDFC Bank)
Darya Ganj, New Delhi-110 002 (INDIA)
Off. © 23260783, 23265523, Res. © 23842660
Fax: 011-23272766
E-mail: manaspublications@vsnl.com
www.manaspublications.in

Second Impression 2010

ISBN 81-7049-289-0
Rs. 495/-

Typeset at
Manas Publications

Printed in India at
RK Offset, Delhi
and Published by Mrs Suman Lata for
Manas Publications, 4402/5-A, Main Ansari F
(Opp. HDFC Bank),
Darya Ganj, New Delhi-110 002 (INDIA)

Contents

Preface

Knowledge is the new currency of this millennium. Knowing the right things at the right time and acting on them with the right amount of energy and effort is critical to personal and professional advancement. It is the mandate of the times we live in that we have to be well-informed and have to have the ability to reach out to the information that we need for our progress. There is a paradigm shift in what brings success in the new 'information age'. One of the most important gains an industry can have is an early insight into the needs, environmental forces and trends that others have not noticed. Being able to perceive an opportunity or a threat and be able to respond to it ahead of others, brings forth a vital competitive advantage. This is precisely what a national intelligence organization does in the context of national security in this world of friends and foes. Successful business and professional organizations are required today to develop many of the skills and approaches that an intelligence organization uses for its own management.

A determination to excel can alone give an individual or an organization an edge which is so vital in the competitive environment that has overtaken us. Change is the one constant in business and personal life now. It is only an 'intelligent' organization that has a clear understanding of its strengths and weaknesses as well as those of the competitors. Competitive intelligence is the ongoing knowledge that such an organization has about the competitors and the competitive conditions. Today the world has become a global village and open information is shared universally as soon as it is produced. The advent of border-less markets, moreover, creates the possibility that your competitor may be there in any part of the globe and not necessarily in your own vicinity. There is no guarantee that your competitive advantage can last long. Competitive intelligence is needed not only to gain an edge but also to retain it. Today the corporate world is increasingly relying on information professionals to act as a think-tank to help out the businesses in the sphere of strategy formulation.

An 'intelligent' business organization garners information, creates knowledge and churns knowledge into innovation. Information of intelligence value is available from open sources but not all information is piled on the 'shelves' or is accessible in published form. It requires skills to reach out to information but it must be remembered that all information gathering must be done within the legal and ethical parameters. It is becoming increasingly evident that competitive intelligence is in a good measure the product of competent business analysis.

Competitive intelligence is information that is produced and retained confidentially. Information of intelligence value has to be protected against the prying attempts of the competitors. Competitive intelligence and business vigilance are therefore the two sides of the same coin. Corporate security means protection of the organization's assets against the unseen threats from outside as also from within. These threats exist in the form of industrial espionage, subversion of the work force and sabotage, and for each of these threats a specific security package has to be put in place.

Today, knowledge is a precious organizational resource. We are, in fact, at the threshold of what can be described as the 'age of intelligence' in which individuals, organizations and nations will be required to have information that can enable them to take decisions with futuristic implications. In other words, they would need 'intelligence' or knowledge that is exclusively their own to move towards their goals and objectives. At the same time, notwithstanding the demands of competitiveness, businesses and professional organizations will need to have well-defined ethical practices. An ethical framework of corporate governance has become important because it enhances internal stability and corporate loyalty and also becomes a source of competitive advantage in the long run.

A nation is a collection of human beings who choose to have a shared identity. A corporate body, likewise, represents a convergence of human activity within an organizational identity. We recognize this organization today as a 'corporate citizen' rightly emphasising its human content. The challenge of change facing the corporate world in the era of globalization, compels a comparison with the framework of Charles Darwin's theory of how life progresses. The Information Age has made the progression irreversible. Movement is the rule whether it leads to success or failure. The corporate growth is evolutionary because it will never be along a beaten path.

Globalization has created a new struggle for existence that is universal. Corporate Darwinism is in full play. Global competitors are the new predators operating on the strength of the cost benefits of scale, technology access and more importantly, the multi-market hedging of risks. The message of this struggle is that there will be survival of the fittest, not necessarily of the strongest. Acting adaptively is what is required to manage change and enhance competitiveness. A smart player in business today realises that it is intelligence that provides strength.

Today business moves fast, product cycles are measured in months not years and partners become rivals in no time. You have to keep an eye on your competitors and since markets have become increasingly global in nature, businesses that want to succeed have to reckon with global competition. The ability to compete in the home market does not ensure success internationally. Organizations which fail to consider their opportunities in the global market-place will go the way of the dinosaur. They need intelligence for success. Skills of intelligence have to be applied in a global setting. Learning about suppliers, customers, regulators and of course competitors gives an enterprise an insight into the future of its business and adds to its ability to adopt a pro-active approach in all aspects of its operations whether it is the marketing strategy, technological upgradation, pricing, packaging or customer appeal.

This book discusses the principles and precepts of competitive intelligence and business vigilance. Business, similar to a career in Intelligence, is all about having information on human thinking and activity. To succeed in either, one requires a deep understanding of human psychology, a logical and analytical mind, and a capacity to respond innovatively to change.

D.C. Pathak

1

The Challenge of Change

- **Pursuit of excellence brings competitive advantage**

The last decade of the Twentieth century changed beyond recognition the geo-political, economic and security scenarios of the world. The Nineties began with an unprecedented sweep that brought about a sudden demise of the USSR, ended the cold-war between the combative ideologies of International Communism and Western Capitalism and ushered in the unipolar world. Around the same time the Information Technology Revolution firmly established the economic globalization that brought new opportunities to the business and professional organizations on the one hand and posed new threats and challenges to settled firms on the other. It gave a new meaning to competitiveness and made it clear that if you gained an edge you had to constantly work to retain it. Finally, the early Nineties laid the foundations of a new kind of global terrorism that was much wider in its base and stronger in its determination than any other source of clandestine violence existing till then. A new motivation rooted in notions of faith and interpretations of religion arose and the resources and arsenal commandeered by the non-state forces transformed this terror into the fountain-head of a new kind of covert warfare.

The terrorist attack on the WTC in New York and the Pentagon in Washington on September 11, 2001 caused an adverse impact on the US and world economy and affected the doctrines of war. It undermined the efficacy of the mathematical models of business analysis and compelled a switch-over to 'alternate scenarios' for futuristic assessments. Firms that dealt with new methods of identification and authentication, such as those exploring biometrics, gained a new-found importance. A new world order, the advent of border-less markets and the widespread vulnerability to global terrorism, combined to produce the new dynamics of change, which is continuing to challenge individuals, organizations and the nation-states alike. The war on Iraq carried out by the Anglo-American combine in March 2003, was justified on the new doctrine of pre-emption. It was different from war as a defensive response. Intelligence on Iraq had not clearly established a hostile 'move' or 'plan' of Iraq against the US or the UK, beyond tentative evidence that Iraq in the past had some biological and chemical 'weapons of mass destruction.' In the unipolar world, this approach to the issues of war and peace is another change of far-reaching significance to which the nation-states have to find a suitable response.

The challenge of change can be met, among other things, by being well-informed which means that you have the right information at the right time and in the context of business investment, at the right price too. It also means that you have the information that makes a difference between a decision and a guess because this can be the difference between success and failure and hence between wealth and poverty. It is the right decision taken at the right time that determines success. Moreover, being well informed means being continuously informed since the competition is also continual. Being updated is not a one-time event. Today's firms need people who are information savvy. Such people have traits in common with the members of an Intelligence organization. They tend to read a lot and try to preserve information through subject categorization. They have an unsatiable curiosity arising out of a spirit of inquiry which propels them to try to find out more about any matter. Since business information is largely about human planning and activity, such people have a healthy interest in human psychology and behaviour. Information savvy executives have a certain ability to interact with and handle people at the place of work and out-side.

Further, such executives look for information of quality, or in other words, information that has credibility and utility. They have a natural tendency to prefer an authoritative opinion to gossip, and have the ability to identify the useful information as against what is unimportant. They distinguish the essentials from non-essentials in any situation because they have an analytical mind that can see a thing in its larger perspective. It is this ability that keeps them from the affliction called 'information overload' or 'information anxiety.' The most important characteristic of an information conscious executive is that he has the discipline of a logical progression of thought. This helps him or her to formulate the right questions during the quest for information – what is needed ? where can we get it from ? and how can that information be accessed ? In an age where timely information leads to right action, half the battle is won if the 'problem' or the 'task' can be correctly defined.

In the information age changes are sudden and swift. Today business is conducted with unprecedented speed. Mobile phones, PC networks, Fax, e-mail and overnight delivery services have all lent incredible pace to transactions. Technological and social developments have combined to make life brisk. Information is shared as soon as it is created. Dow Jones provides worldwide financial coverage that is as current as 30 seconds. There is a new level of competitiveness. Your competitor may confront you from any distance because globalization has removed geographical and national boundaries separating markets. The monitoring of competitors is a major determinant of progress in business. Many leading companies in the USA employ staff specifically for this purpose.

The dynamics of change for a business organization revolve round three players — the firm, its rivals, and the external determinants under which they all operate. Apart from keeping track of the competitor's thinking and activity, a business has to watch the competitive conditions. Study of variables in the competitive environment is a must if a firm hopes to take the right business decisions. The factors range from politico-legal regimen to demographic changes like increase in the population of senior citizens, pattern of family structure and so on.

In an era driven by change retaining a competitive advantage would be made possible only by using a strategy that ensures, first and foremost, a balance between anarchy and order or between rapid shifts and stability. The firm has to embrace change and not skirt it and yet move forward. Change is both a threat and an opportunity. Propelled by information technology and globalization, new products and services are appearing at the market-place everyday and your firm could either be among their creators or be left defending your brand against them. The age of information is setting off a new economic evolution in which those who creatively adapt to the new scenario would survive and grow. The 'intelligent' firm will not be put down by a setback because it knows that no failure or gain is permanent and that a constant change brings in new opportunities as well.

It is the ability to anticipate a change, whether in the line-up of products in the market, in the competitive environment, or in the customer demands, that can convert the implicit threat into a gainful response. The challenge of change, however, lies in the organization becoming pro-active about accepting change as a reality. Such an enterprise spends a significant part of its organizational energy on probing into the possible value additions that can be made in its operations and structure and the extent of innovative thinking that can be brought into play for creating better versions of its products and services.

The challenge of change will compel business firms to seek survival strategies that are so characteristically adopted by species facing the forces of evolution. An ongoing adaptation to change, rather than an attempt to stall the change, will be the hallmark of the strategy. Like some animals in the wild hunting in packs, the firms may be inclined to come together selectively to take mutual advantage of each other. Businesses may also practice symbiosis which is a limited convergence of two independent organizations for gaining from the strength of each other. Collaboration between brands for joint marketing is one simple example of this phenomenon. In a situation of constant change, a firm would do well to put its inherited experience of the past into use, examine the present environment and consider new options for moving ahead. Competitive intelligence will help it to take right decisions and succeed in the same way as advancing species do in the matter of picking up the choices in the evolutionary process of 'natural selection.' At the same time, conscious attempts by firms to innovate would bring success just as creating 'mutations' or random variations speed up this advance in appropriate cases. Businesses are live organisms and much of what happens to their growth is presaged by the quality of human thinking and initiatives they are able to rally for their operations.

It is a part of the challenge of change that we must be able to make decisions even with incomplete information. This does not detract from the basic merit of knowledge-based action. We will often face a situation where things are not totally clear. Ambiguity is something we have to learn to live with while conducting business. This may happen even in other spheres of life. We should not let it create too much discomfort for us.

Conclusion

Globalization hastened by the advent of the information age, has posed a new kind of challenge to all those businesses which take their existing advantage for granted. Firms are exposed to changes that may be sudden and swift — altering the profile of the competitors as well as the competitive environment on any of the innumerable counts. Today a successful business organization has to be well-informed about the potential shifts in the market scene and be pro-active about accepting the challenge of change. The challenge is enormous because globalization has created border-less markets. A business enterprise, if it wants to be in the competition for success, should adapt to change and not seek to stall or skirt it.

2

Information and Intelligence

- **Being updated is not a one-time event**

If in the age of knowledge it is mandatory that you have to be well-informed for being successful, then it is necessary also to understand what 'Information' is. In simplest terms, information can be described as data or facts that convey a meaning and tell you something that you did not already know. Unless a fact is meaningful, it does not measure up to the definition of 'Information.' However, what it conveys may be information for you but not necessarily for your competitor who has already had access to it. Information thus lays the foundation of competitive advantage.

Knowledge is collated information that sets the degree of your being well-informed about a subject or sphere. It is in-depth information in a particular direction. Knowledge is the instrument of specialization. A specialist knows the facts of his subject embedded in the past. He matches them with what is going on in the present and uses the outcome along with other collateral evidence to evaluate or assess what might happen in the times to come. Organizations which are looking ahead, therefore do need specialists who essentially put together and analyse information of the past and the present to try to get a peep into the future. An intelligence organization, as is well known, procures information that can help to get the futuristic picture. It employs area and subject specialists to assist analysis. What is basically common between a classical intelligence organization and a business corporation in the competitive environ is that both are trying to see what the future has in store for them.

What is Intelligence ? Intelligence is a kind of information. All intelligence is information but all information is not intelligence. Intelligence is information that satisfies a certain collectivity of parameters. First, intelligence is all about human thinking and activity. Information may be there in the form of statistics about the country's mineral wealth, water resources or the density of population. An awareness of the names of the members of the Cabinet at the helm of a democratic governance is information, but knowledge of who amongst them exercise a veto on policy decisions is of intelligence value. Names of members of the Board of Directors of a company is information but the process by which board decisions are taken is intelligence. To get this information it would become necessary to identify the key decision makers who may not have found a place in the recorded information. A basic commonality between an intelligence organization and a business corporation is that both are concerned with human activity. They both are keen to know what the individuals heading the competitor's or the adversary's establishment are planning and doing. In both cases, a good knowledge of human thinking and behaviour becomes a requirement for success.

Once the human content of intelligence is understood, it is not difficult to grasp its second dimension: intelligence is information that gives an idea of the unseen 'hostile' moves emanating from the camp of the 'rival' or the 'adversary.' Your opponent may, infact, be covertly trying to get at what is happening on your side and to reach out to your own secrets. In other words, the 'enemy' may be indulging in 'espionage' which in the context of corporate business and industry is called 'industrial espionage.' Another form of 'invisible' attack from the adversary may be by way of his attempts to damage the loyalty of your work-force which is broadly what can be described as 'subversion.' The 'enemy' may even be planning to cause outright destruction of your assets without showing his hand, which is what 'sabotage' is. Sabotage means 'unacceptable' physical damage. It may range from destruction of machinery to an attack on the information system of the enterprise.

From this second dimension of intelligence follows its third parameter which is that intelligence is information that has to be obtained and handled confidentially. The competitor or the adversary does not want the other side to know what his moves are. Intelligence is, therefore, information about the rival's surreptitious or hidden plans and activity. If you are collecting information about these, then this has to be done in a manner that the opponent does not come to know what you have learnt about his moves. Your knowledge about your rival or adversary then becomes your own confidential information or intelligence. Intelligence gives you the advantage so long as its confidentiality is preserved. It becomes, infact, your proprietary information which you must protect. If you have not kept your trade secrets and confidential information 'protected', you can not blame the opponent for indulging in 'espionage' against your firm. Espionage, by definition, is 'unauthorized access to protected information.' If the proprietor has not protected his information, accessing it in the public domain is everybody's right. Protection of information is done through a system of security classification by which the material is marked as 'confidential', 'restricted' or 'for internal use only.' The labels 'secret' and 'top secret' are normally used by the agencies of the State. Restriction of access to confidential information has to be defined by the firm by laying down 'authorization' procedures. To sum up, intelligence is information about intended industrial espionage, subversion and sabotage directed against your establishment. A classical intelligence organization collects this information pertaining to the nation's enemies. In the context of competitive intelligence in the business world, it is information about the moves being planned in the rival camp.

The fourth parameter of intelligence is determined by yet another definition of intelligence according to which 'intelligence is information for action.' Intelligence is information that prevents a mishap or indicates an opportunity and hence it must be made available before the time to act on it is over. Intelligence is not a post-event analysis but information that indicates what is likely to happen or what lies ahead. This is why information of intelligence value has to be communicated with speed to the action taking or decision-making authority. Prompt communication of intelligence is as important as the intelligence itself. Failures can result if the information, though available, is not passed on to the decision-makers in time or when action is not taken on the intelligence that is made available. Handling business intelligence, therefore, is a function that should be performed right under the supervision of the top management.

Many Fortune companies in the US and Europe now engage business information professionals to collect, collate and analyze information to produce competitive intelligence. Intelligence for business basically focuses on reliable internal information on competitors and competitive conditions.

Last but not the least, intelligence is in most cases synonymous with analyzed information. Even business information received from open sources can be churned into competitive intelligence by competent professionals. A classical intelligence organization that works for national security also has a lot of information collected from the public domain. Broad contours of a 'threat' can be perceived on the basis of open information. However, only when this information is put together with 'intelligence' secured through special skills or the trade-craft of the profession, that the threat is brought into focus and seen in its time-frame. This time-frame is vital as it enables the decision-makers to formulate the character and timing of the 'response' or 'action.' In the complex world of today when the enemy's plans cannot be presented on a platter even by the resourceful combination of human and technical intelligence of a high order, the function of analysis as the instrument of intelligence generation is becoming important. In the competitive world of business also a lot comes out of sound business analysis even as intelligence professionals trained in the skills of collecting inside information are now beginning to occupy an important place there. It is not so much a cloak-and-dagger stuff in business but use of intelligence skills, nevertheless, does have a definite place in a firm. The importance of competitive intelligence will increase since the same open information is now becoming available to all players at the same time. Competitive advantage can now be gained only from 'intelligence.'

Conclusion

In the age of knowledge, competitive advantage comes to those who are well-informed. Information that helps an enterprise to take a futuristic decision to its exclusive advantage can be categorized as intelligence. This information can either come from confidential channels or sources or it can be churned out of the facts available in the open, through a competent analysis. Intelligence basically is information that indicates an opportunity that lies ahead or unearths the signs of an impending threat or a problem. In either case, it calls for a quick response. Failure to act on intelligence can expose the organization to an avoidable setback. Since intelligence is your exclusive or proprietary information, it should be handled confidentially and kept protected atleast till such time as is needed for action. Since information technology revolution has made it possible for everyone to access the same information in the public domain, the importance of intelligence for competitive advantage is increasing everyday.

3

Accessing Information

- **What is known cannot become unknown but it can be superseded by new information.**

In the age of knowledge, those who are better attuned to garnering information that is significant for them, have a better chance of succeeding in their mission. They are pro-active in reaching out to a source of knowledge. They know the rule that 'you have to find information, information does not find you.' They work with the conviction that information sought by them is almost certainly available somewhere. They launch their quest for information with a logical mind and have their own thoughts crystallized around questions like What is it that they are looking for? Where possibly could that information be available? And how can they reach the source that can give them that information? They are quick to check out on what is already available to them in-house at their own organization's resource centre. They realize that information not in the public domain may have to be obtained by using special skills. They are aware that professional help of investigators and surveyors may have to be taken in suitable cases.

Those who run business organizations should also know that information is never free. Knowledge creation needs investment. Information gathering, however, should on principle be made cost-effective. One way of doing this is to develop the ability to see what is relevant and important and distinguish it from all that is not significant.

The package of attitudinal traits outlined above is built into a successful information seeker. These are, infact, among the prerequisites that the members of a classical intelligence organization are expected to have. Today's firm has to have the attributes of an 'intelligent' organization to stay on in the lead.

Remember, there is a wealth of information available within and outside your organization. A large proportion of business information required for taking strategic decisions is available from open sources ranging from published material to the organized think-tanks who openly carry out incisive studies of various facets of the business world. There are also information gathering services ranging from on-line data base providers to those who carry out contracted studies. Information drawn from 'open' sources if subjected to collation and analysis, can yield information of intelligence value. Competitive intelligence is information that exclusively helps your firm to take futuristic decisions on its business operations, expansion or reorganization.

The published material has an enormous range. There are reference guides and company directories. There is a publication on just about any trade. Many trade publications come out with special issues that contain valuable information. Published material, however, may not be up to date. A company may overstate or understate its sales figures. Business news on television channels or in newspapers is useful but it may suffer from over-interpretation or sensationalism. There are published market studies. Research firms produce growth forecasts or reports on market size. They are available at a price. They are not reliable in absolute terms and, infact, they should be treated as an educated guess that needs to be independently corroborated. As regards think-tanks who conduct business analysis, a prudent approach would be to accept their facts but not necessarily their findings.

The governments themselves are among the biggest information providers. Besides, there are various kinds of Associations like medical association, automobile association and association of engineers and they provide extremely useful information. University and college libraries are excellent resource centres of information. Special libraries are also located in businesses or management institutions.

The most productive way of accessing open information is to reach out to the on-line data base providers. It should never be forgotten, however, that the information available on the internet is not necessarily trustworthy. Cyber-space reveals what has been fed to the computers. It does not guarantee truthfulness of the information provided on-line. There are Gateway Services whose 'menu' system makes an automatic search in response to the specific questions posed to it. The Services charge for information retrieval. Businesses can take help of firms that act as 'information brokers' for locating information on their behalf. Remember that insufficient updating is a common flaw in many on-line data bases.

Mention may also be made of the agencies which undertake studies of businesses on contract. These are firms that carry out 'custom' studies and reviews ordered by a client. The results belong to the client exclusively. These firms can conduct primary research through interviews and surveys for a charge and have the expertise to use technical tools like 'random sampling error' or 'non-response error' in conducting a poll. The client should be knowledgeable about the pitfalls of contracted research such as selective pickup of data or what is called 'massaging' of information to fit into the findings. The bottom line for those in the quest of information is that they should always use their own intelligence.

Last but not the least, a firm can take the help of investigative services for obtaining competitive intelligence. There are companies that prepare investigative reports on corporations and executives. In the West, their operations are fairly well developed. They stand on the border-line between the fields of openly available information and the knowledge gained through the 'special skills' used for securing information in a covert way but within legal parameters.

Easy access to information is resulting in the new phenomenon of all systems and individuals running into 'information overload.' The time that is taken for sifting information is at the cost of productivity. Minimising this avoidable waste of time and energy in garnering the right information is a line of development that information technology has to address now. This can be done firstly by building features of analysis into the exercise of 'search' itself. The Ws – What, Why and Where– of accessing information have to be better defined. Secondly, the information made available has to be subjected to a simultaneous analytical sieve to mark the significant from the less important, on the basis of the given parameters. Thirdly, it should be possible to do some collation on the spot. Information technology is already making it feasible to do on-line sharing of the accessed information with others concerned, at work.

In all businesses and professions today, knowledge has become a crucial organizational resource. Strategic decisions rest on reliable information. Those engaged in pursuit of information must note the guidelines that would bring them success. Remember that information does not find you; you have to reach out to it. You have to have the initiative to find the place or the person where or with whom the information is located. Presume that the information you seek will be found with proper effort. A positive mind-set and a sense of optimism must motivate you. Intelligence professionals work with the presumption that they would get what they are looking for. They never feel cowed down by fears of failure. Securing information needs time and energy and the leadership of an organization or business house must have arrangements and systems to check upon the information of relevance that is available within the outfit's own internal resource or record before permitting an investment for obtaining it from a source outside. Remember, also, that information is never free. Procurement of information, however, should be cost-effective to the extent possible. Information savvy people have the right questions in mind when they embark on the mission of knowledge generation. They know what they are looking for and also what information is useful.

It is surprising how most people have little idea of what to do to find out what they need to know. It is so common to see top executives afflicted with 'information anxiety' resulting from their inability to cope up with the information flow. They lose their grit and clarity for decision-making and run the risk of missing out on the right strategy formulation within the optimal limits of time. Information handling in a scenario of high competition needs skills that do not grow on everybody. It needs qualities like inter-active capability, presence of mind, and an analytical intellect. To get, out of the information available to everybody, something that has special significance for your organization, is the core competence of intelligence professionals. Today, competitive intelligence of good value, generally comes out of sound analysis. Success in business becomes easier if the firm is headed by people who can strategize on the basis of opportunities and threats revealed by such intelligence.

An intelligent organization creates an effective information gathering system. A prime requirement in the context of a business organization is to keep updating the information not only about the competitors but also on products, market trends, government regulations and other factors of competitive environment. Overseeing the information gathering system is a top management function. It can be delegated only to an information executive at the apex with overall responsibility for all the information resources of the organization – both internal and external. Such an information manager must establish an information centre which in turn can have a library of reference materials and a computer terminal for accessing data bases. Many firms do not care even to subscribe to the principal professional magazines of their field of business. They are not aware that conferences are a good source of information and competitive intelligence. They do not even have arrangements to regularly talk to their customers. Beyond using casual contacts and relying on advisors, they do not build any system for information gathering with the result that they lose out in competition just for an avoidable inadequacy of knowledge.

It is necessary to make a distinction between internal and external information. In a business context, internal information involves facts about your own company whereas external information is what relates to the world outside. Facts about competitors, markets, demographies, environment, etc. which constitute external information, are difficult to obtain. Companies are known to have suffered because they failed to take note of changes in the market-place or demographies.

An integral examination of the data available internally on the company's competitors and the external information gathered from information suppliers outside, is the major responsibility of the information executive at the top. The latter can, depending upon the size of the enterprise, create a nucleus of persons at the information centre who know how to collect information, how to disseminate it and how to keep it on record for use in the future. The information executive should have the authority to receive external information from the company's own marketing, sales and research divisions as also the discretion to hire for a fee, the services of information consultants or 'brokers' who are in the business of running their own data bases and surveys. Some alternative information delivery technologies are gaining ground. CD-ROM (compact disk – read only memory) is becoming popular. It involves one-time investment in place of the hourly on-line charges. The material is also more comprehensive which is an advantage. On-line data bases however should not be presumed to be the only evidence of the existence of information that is being sought. Importance of sources other than these will remain important. Even while using on-line data the methodology of intelligence should be followed which means that an independent confirmation of the information retrieved on-line should be obtained particularly on points that are crucial for decision-making.

The better informed you are, the easier it becomes for you to decide how exactly to put any new information to good business use. As already mentioned information gathering begins with the formulation of the right kind of questions. The harder part is to think about ways of securing information that is not easily available. Information gathering is easier if the quest is focused on specific objectives and intelligible questions. If the requirement is defined in terms of what information you need and what you will do with it, sourcing for it will also become a shade clearer. The information you are seeking may not be on the 'shelves.' It may have to be collected first hand by organizing a survey or using confidential techniques. Finding information is a skill that can be acquired through training and hands-on experience. Successful business persons need education on the subject of information. In the age of knowledge, assumptions and guesses cannot substitute for information. To seek information on something that you do not know is never a reflection on your basic abilities. No question of ego is involved at all if you are seen to be filling the gaps in your information. In fact, it is a positive trait of your personality that you accept only an authentic and complete picture and discount presumptions.

Inadequacy of information-gathering and not the dearth of available information is often the reason why a business enterprise fails to take the right decisions. In today's world the leaders of trade and industry have to be information savvy. They are not frightened of confronting too much information and they have the instinctive ability to note what is relevant and significant. They are willing to read and absorb a brief. They can take work out of those who are skilled in the business of information-gathering. Both, information collectors and information users, have to have the sense of distinguishing the essentials from the non-essentials and not permitting the volume of facts and data flowing in to swamp them. A perceptive and analytical mind is a prerequisite for successfully dealing with information at any level in an organization.

Conclusion

Information savvy executives proactively seek out the source of knowledge that can give them what they are looking for. If the information is not on the 'shelves' they press into service those who can use special skills to ferret out that information or build the futuristic picture by analyzing whatever has been accessed through open channels. The enterprise should avoid resort to methods of collecting information that are outside the legal and ethical parameters. Establishing reliability of the information received is of crucial importance as acting on wrong information can cause greater damage than the possible disadvantage resulting from lack of information. Information gathering should be cost-effective and geared to the objective in view. Firms today need executives who can create and handle an effective information gathering system without getting debilitated by 'information overload.'

4

Skills For Gathering Intelligence

- **Competitive Intelligence is needed not only to gain an edge but also to retain it.**

Today information has become a sustaining force for any business. A modern business enterprise needs information for its health, in a similar manner as the flow of blood that is required to support life. Business intelligence serves many vital needs of a firm. It is only on the basis of correct and complete information that an enterprise can determine its monopolistic leverage. Information is required to prepare backgrounders on the contacts from whom facts about the competition can be obtained. Collation of government related knowledge and information about other elements of the competitive environment is important. Information helps a firm to visualize new opportunities and foresee any major troubles ahead. It is needed to formulate strategies and policies to meet the specific objectives of the enterprise and subsequently to make a mid-course correction, if necessary. Information helps to reach right decisions on product price and product diversification and to determine allocation of capital resources. Internally, the firm has to have complete information to exercise control over its business operations and to keep up the performance of the management, particularly in a situation where the firm operates on a global scale. Lastly, corporate security itself is based on information and cost-effective procedures to safeguard it can be framed only on the strength of internal and external knowledge available to the enterprise.

Not all information is available on-line or in published form. A whole lot of facts that you are seeking lie dormant as tacit knowledge with the people whom you may or may not be in contact with. You may have to identify such people, find a way of reaching them and get them to talk to you about the matter you are interested in. The information needed by you may be a part of the knowledge resource of another firm. If this firm is a competitor it may be keeping that information protected with the label of confidentiality. Accessing somebody's protected information without his or her consent or authority, may amount to a violation of legal parameters. Stealing trade secrets is described as 'industrial espionage,' which is not only an act that is unsavoury but is something that will invite legal action.

Quite often it would be the case that you have a lot of data and facts from open sources and you have subjected them to a competent analysis to cull out information that is vital for your business plans. Obviously this is the information that you would keep to your own self atleast till your plans have been put into operation. You are in possession of information which has the attributes of intelligence. Intelligence, by definition, is reliable information that helps you to take a decision which brings you competitive advantage and is required to be handled confidentially. Information that exclusively serves your interest in this manner is in professional terms called 'competitive intelligence.' Building competitive intelligence through analysis or procuring it through the use of special skills for gathering intelligence, is increasingly becoming a professional endeavour. Large firms are now quite willing to invest on professionals to collect, collate and analyze information to produce competitive intelligence.

Ferreting out information from individuals who are in possession of it but not willing to part with the facts, however, is a kind of skill that can be developed. Intelligence professionals do it all the time. The skills for gathering intelligence can be cultivated in a general sense by people in any line of business for whom the need to have information about competitors and competitive environment becomes important for their own legitimate advancement. These skills basically rest on the ability to befriend people and influence them into sharing information with you: on the art of conducting 'interviews' with people from whom you are hoping to get the information of your interest; and on an understanding of what is called in the professional parlance as the use of a legitimate 'cover' for collecting information. Remember that a cover alters your 'placing' or 'purpose' but not your 'identity.' If you lie about your identity and pretend to be someone else you make yourself vulnerable to the charge of impersonation. In any case, any such attempt would tend to block your business activities conducted in your real identity. You may on occasions need for your business, information that is not there on the 'shelf' but is with somebody who can be accessed only through a special effort. You need this vital missing link in the information chain to enable you to take a strategic or futuristic stand about your business. This piece of information you need so badly will perhaps come only by using skills of intelligence gathering.

Good intelligence basically comes from human contacts. Successful firms make arrangements for a systematic exchange of business information not only with their own departmental managers and consultants but also with their workers at the grass roots. Interaction with customers, suppliers, bankers and brokers also yields useful intelligence. Information managers try to find out if the company's ex-employees, engaged with other organizations, can provide any useful knowledge. The people who have access to the competitors can be approached too. On-site contractors and ad-agencies handling the competitor's work fall in this category. The former employees of a competitor can also be contacted. Mergers among the firms can create a situation of flux. The potential for collecting information from the employees being laid off, can be legitimately exploited. Your own friends in the market outside are of course the more easily approachable contacts.

Creation of a human source of information involves three crucial steps. First of all, you have to identify and locate the person who can give you information that you are seeking about the competition. Once this is done, you have to find a way of approaching him if he is not acquainted with you at all. An appropriate and natural looking introduction is followed by a period, short or long in which the contact is personally cultivated. This is done by extending hospitality and other favours. He learns to attach importance to your friendship and feels completely at ease about discussing his area of work with you. If he has just left the enterprise which you are interested in knowing about, he would be freely talking about its inner working. If, however, he is still on its rolls, you have to be careful not to ask for facts whose revelation will make him uncomfortable. The objective of raising a human informant is to instill in him a degree of confidence in his friendship with you so that he reveals to you certain matters without harbouring any fear of running into difficulty on that count. He does so as he feels obliged enough to meet your need for that information, out of the sense of importance that he gives to your friendship. A disgruntled employee of any organization is more willing to talk about the inner irregularities or goings-on in his establishment to the outsiders.

Much of the need for accessing human sources of information in the area of competitive intelligence can, however, be met through social interactions, skillful use of meetings and conferences, utilization of training courses for executives, exploitation of contacts made in course of trade fairs, business interviews, and circulation of business questionnaires for a feed-back from customers. It is reported that the Central Intelligence Agency warned US aerospace companies of a suspected plot by the French foreign intelligence service to lure them to the 1993 Paris Air Show, implicitly for espionage purposes.[1]

In intelligence parlance, information of value can be had from the so-called 'unconscious agents.' These are people who can be drawn into a discussion about their work, in social and professionals meets, once they develop a sense of closeness with you. This closeness may arise from a feeling of 'common identity' rooted in caste, region, similar likes and dislikes, or even a comparable family structure. 'Social engineering' techniques are often used by information seekers to create such a rapport with others. Scientists and technology experts often like to talk about their current research to patient and interested listeners. If you present yourself as a keen student of science, you can prompt a scientist to explain the line of his research to you. In an intelligence organization, the hands-on experience of one member in the use of skills of intelligence gathering becomes useful knowledge for the others. The organization attaches a lot of importance to case studies on the execution of these skills and uses them for its own training programmes.

It may be mentioned again that it is unethical and even violative of the legal parameters, for any firm to attempt to steal away the trade secrets or an employee of the rival business house. Use of 'bribery' or 'blackmail' in doing so can lead to serious consequences. However, an open offer of a job with higher compensations, made through a legitimate public announcement, even if done with an eye on a professional of the competitor's camp, cannot be objected to. Interviewing the applicants drawn from the rival companies for the purpose of gleaning information of interest about the competitive situation, is a fair game provided the advertisement for the job itself has no fakeness of any sort around it. This is one reason why firms have their own protective 'exit policy' in respect of the employees leaving them for positions elsewhere.

Information brokers and investigative services are a growing profession in the sphere of competitive intelligence. Such agencies use special skills like surveillance, confidential inquiries and legitimate use of technical gadgetry to carry out their contracted study or an investigative assignment. The art of surveillance is in watching a target without his or her knowledge. In a public place everybody has a right to observe everybody else but if the target comes to know that he or she is under watch, the objective of the operation is lost. The watcher therefore is advised to see that he merges into the background. He should avoid wearing gaudy clothes and should use a footwear that does not cause discomfiture in long walks necessitated by the assignment. At a finer level of proficiency, he should have a good idea of the area where he is operating and should have the presence of mind to give a logical reason for his being present at that place and time. The right of use of a public place is different from a tresspass into any private premises, and the watcher certainly does not have any authority to tamper with anything belonging to the individual under watch. There is a clear dividing line between the skillful and the unlawful as far as the ways of collecting information on the quiet are concerned.

Confidential inquiries are different from an open investigation. The latter can be done only on the authority of the State and is therefore, reserved as a function only for the agencies that work on behalf of the State to prevent crime and disorder. Individuals and institutions have the right to carry out their own personal inquires confidentially without encroaching on the rights of anybody else. Checking up on the antecedents of an employee or a partner in a potential joint venture, is legitimate for a firm. A confidential inquiry has to be a planned affair. The goal of intelligence has to be defined. Several steps may be required to complete the inquiry. The project may need a combination of skills like approaching an informant, watching somebody or holding an interview under 'cover.' It is necessary to ascertain what part of information is already available within the organization's resource centre and on the 'shelves' outside. Since the skills for gathering information confidentially require investment, the competitive intelligence obtained should be commensurate with the funds used. The value of intelligence often is computed in terms of the cost that the firm will incur in case it did not have the benefit of that information. All intelligence gathering must be made cost-effective.

Getting people to open up to you in an interview and provide you with information that is not available elsewhere, is an important skill that should be mastered by those who are in the business of gathering competitive intelligence. The art of interviewing can be perfected by following certain do's and dont's. The interview should begin with a friendly conversation in which there is no drilling and a casual tone is maintained. If you volunteer something of value, without of course giving out anything confidential about your own firm, it might become easier for you to draw out the other person on information that you would like to have in exchange. This is not a barter but a method of putting you and the interviewee on the same side of the fence. The interviewer otherwise must act as if he knows very little and let the other person explain more of what he knows. Do not interrupt the interviewee and if the latter stops prematurely, permit the pause. Typically, people try to fill the uncomfortable silences in conversation created by them, on their own.

A competent interviewer asks questions that require longer answers and not just yes or no type of reply. You can ask the same question in different ways. Leading questions should be cleverly slipped in during the middle of the conversation and not in the beginning or at the end. A person is less conscious when the conversation has proceeded for a while but is still not close to its termination. Make mention of rumours or any other tit-bits you have got from elsewhere as a catalyst for inducing the other person to come out with his version. Make use of the post-interview 'small talk' to get at possible revelations. The interviewee may be asked to suggest if any other person could be spoken to or some published material seen by you in the context of the interview. This may provide useful clues. Finally, it is important to study the body language of the other person as this helps you to know and deduce what he has left unsaid. A shrug or a frown may reveal more than the spoken word.

The First Chief Directorate of the KGB in erstwhile USSR reportedly could establish firms run by its own officers for the purpose of collecting corporate intelligence. Chinese nationals working in the US in high-tech research, it is said, were provided free trips home so that the government scientists in China could interact with them and debrief them on their work. The French government was said to be quite willing to help the French firms with resources to get competitive intelligence. On their own, many Fortune companies in the West have intelligence units working under the labels of Strategic Planning, Business Research or Market Analysis. A good illustration is the ABB, the Swedish business giant which reportedly has a full-fledged competitive intelligence and analysis department answerable to the CEO. It studies economic situation, competitive practices, legal and regulatory issues and the new technologies. It also trains the managers in intelligence.

The exercise of intelligence gathering necessitated by the competitive environment facing business today, has to be conducted within the limits of corporate ethics, human morality and legal boundaries. The professionals must observe the company's guidelines as set forth by its legal department. This creates a grid of understanding among the company's employees and a stable image of the firm outside. Do not lie while representing yourself although you can use a legitimate 'cover' by altering your functional placement or creating an excuse for your being there at a given time and place. Do not knowingly press someone to give information if this could jeopardize that person's job or reputation. Do not bribe, do not steal protected information and do not spirit away an employee of the competitor. In the course of an interview, do not deliberately mislead anyone and do not give data like your firm's price policy to a competitor in the process of securing the latter's inner information. Do not tape-record a conversation or plant an 'eavesdropping' device as these are means available only to those agencies that are trying on the authority of the State, to uncover the nation's enemy. These covert means are not available to competing citizens or corporate bodies who are all supposed to operate openly on a level playing field.

Conclusion

An amazing amount of information of intelligence value relevant to a firm's progress lies untapped in the minds of the work force of that enterprise. A smart business leader finds a way of bringing this out to the firm's advantage before he proceeds to exploit the sources of information outside. Skills of intelligence gathering can be learnt by those who have an analytical mind and certain basic abilities for interacting with and befriending people, not letting their ego affect their approach, and distinguishing the important from the less significant. Importance of competitive intelligence has opened up a new line of profession in which investigative services are made available for obtaining information on corporate bodies and their executives or studies of businesses are undertaken on contract.

Reference

1. *Chicago Tribune,* 29-30 August 1993.

5

Globalization and Intelligence

- **Information is the new raw material which leads to new products, services and marketing strategies.**

It is interesting that the termination of the fierce ideological battle between International Communism and the Western Capitalism marking the advent of a unipolar world in 1991, brought the issue of economic security to the forefront in the foreign policy agenda of the United States. The American hegemony in the global politics and economy has predictably been on the rise since the end of the Cold War. What has aided this process, among other things, is the doctrine enunciated by Warren Christopher, Bill Clinton's Secretary of State in 1993 to the effect that "for the US, national security was inseparable from its economic security[1]." A new meaning and priority was given to economic intelligence which became the instrument for facilitating the increasing involvement of the US economy with the rest of the world, to the advantage of the former. There was talk of the new economic challenges for the Intelligence community of the US. The doctrine of economic security was a pro-active effort of the only super power of the world to strengthen American competitiveness at the international market place.

According to Louis J. Freeh, a former Director of FBI, the agency found that in a surprising number of cases, foreign governments – many of them known to be among the friends of the US – instructed their intelligence services to go after and secure trade secrets that would give their own companies a decided advantage over American competitors. According to him, the FBI identified about forty-three nations that were so instructing their security services and, in most cases, using their own US embassies as bases of operation.[2]

The onset of globalization has produced two new challenges to policy formulation for all major countries. One is to make the concept of national security more comprehensive by integrating the domestic and foreign security issues with economic concerns and the other is to expand the ambit of information-gathering to cover and monitor developments and trends that may potentially harm the national economy. The CIA was already in the business of understanding new technologies that were being developed around the world specially those that had a dual use. A new trend-setter was the access reportedly given to corporate America to the intelligence relevant to the US national economic capabilities available with the government. At the same time, the intelligence agencies were to expand their 'counter-espionage' turf to include the defence of proprietary information and business secrets against theft or unauthorized access. The extent to which the intelligence community in the US directly assisted the American companies in handling their own industrial counter-espionage is, however, difficult to define.

Globalization has made the competitiveness of a country's business a determinant of the nation's economic growth and hence of the national security itself. Nations are going to be competitive even as friends and the support of the national government to the country's business will remain a reality. Information on international competitive environment available to the government, regardless of the sources it comes from, will in some way be put to use for the economic advancement of the nation. Global economy will therefore bring the national government and the country's corporate world together in a manner that does not jeopardize international relations. The role of the national government in safeguarding the country's economic interests is acquiring a new dimension.

An interesting case study in this regard, is the direct intervention of the government of Luxembourg to stall the hostile takeover of its steel giant, Arcelor, initiated by the London-based Indian billionaire Lakshmi N. Mittal, through a $ 23 billion bid. The Luxembourg Prime Minister candidly announced his opposition to the Mittal bid and talked of bringing up a legislation that would allow the companies to decide on takeovers without referral to shareholders. According to a report, Guy Dolle, Chief Executive of Arcelor also ordered the hiring of private detectives to dig dirt on Mittal as part of the Company's all-out fight against the takeover.[3]

Economy is likely to guide political responses in a major way. It is said that the US campaign against Iraq in March 2003 came after a scramble had already begun for Iraq's oil amongst the American, British, French and the Russian national interests. The US war on Iraq, it is widely believed, was a quest for economic consolidation pursued through military means. Imperialism of the past could thus be acquiring an economic definition.

The post-Cold War era incidentally has seen more conflicts arising out of cultural fault-lines than was expected. It has to be seen if the progress of globalization generates new pressures on the politically sovereign entities. These may lead to conflict and war provoked by perceptions that the level playing field was being eliminated and that stronger players were unfairly exploiting the borderless markets.

The emergence of European Union – notwithstanding its newer internal problems – marked a new high in the willingness of like-minded nations to unite for economic gains rather than for military advantage. To compete internationally, nations are forging a new kind of alliance that compares with joint ventures established by corporate entities. Competitiveness of nations is going to be determined by the deftness with which issues of economic health are reconciled with the protection of political sovereignty. In the uni-polar world, the US is in the driver's seat as far as its capacity to invoke its armed might anywhere in the world is concerned. Its economic thrust may make it more intolerant of the road-blocks created by other governments against the march of Corporate America. The intelligence community will step in to help the US government to identify the pressures exerted by rival countries – financial or otherwise – to win over contracts against American businesses. In short, globalization has put new responsibilities on nations in the area of economic policy. India has to handle the reality of an internal disparity of human development on the one hand and prepare for international competitiveness on the other.

A deeper examination of the role of the nation in safeguarding not only its political sovereignty but also its economic independence has become necessary. Globalzsation should not detract from the importance of the nation's political initiatives. The government can ensure that a lot of competitive advantage comes through to the firms from their home ground. Global economy demands interdependence which, however, can operate only amongst partners who are fully independent themselves in terms of their capacity to deliver and ability to understand the expectations of the others. The nation has to sustain its sovereignty in the face of economic globalization and strengthen the enterprises born and brought up on its soil so that they can together handle the competition with the world outside. The politically sovereign nation, however, has the right to adjudicate on the unhealthy practices that any corporation may be tempted to adopt by putting its interests above the concerns of the country. Economic security needs economic intelligence and this new frontier of intelligence should enable the nation to conduct some sort of random vigilance exercise in relation to the companies operating within its frontiers. When a business corporation collapses on account of unethical practices, the nation's economy is hurt. This is no different from some inimical elements causing a setback to the internal security of the nation.

The interdependence of nations fostered by global economy is further reinforced by the compulsions of global security. The success of the anti-Soviet armed campaign in Afghanistan paved the way for the disintegration of the USSR and the demise of International Communism. From the complexities of Afghanistan, however, arose a new terror that provided the run-up to the events of 9/11 and created a new security scenario beset with the global threat of asymmetric warfare. India is aboard the US-led coalition of the willing against the new global terror in line with her belief that illicit guns threatening democratic societies deserve to be neutralized. More than the economic give and take, the comity of democratic nations have to collaborate with each other in countering terrorism and infact in dealing with all forces of covert violence. Since terrorists have trans-national operations and international networking, there has to be a global co-operation in the area of exchange of intelligence required for counter-terrorism effort. Economic security is inseparable from national security and national security is inseparable from international peace. In the age of globalization, all nations have to upgrade their information gathering systems both for economic well-being as well as for security.

The lead has been taken by the US where the CIA Director, Porter Goss, declared that 'our national interests and our security needs are global' and added 'we are going to be in places people can't even imagine'. An enormous territorial spread of the CIA's spy network is underway following the verdict of a blue-ribbon presidential commission there, that the US-led 2003 invasion of Iraq was largely based on bogus intelligence received through foreign intelligence services.[4]

The new challenge for the nation's policy makers is to protect the interests of the domestic business without becoming partial in favour of one or the other sections of the country's own private sector. If ethics in business and corporate governance is acknowledged as being of crucial significance even in a setting of global competition, then the role of the nation's political leadership in safeguarding the economic interests of the nation and, in particular, providing a level playing field to the country's own business enterprises acquires a new importance. It is not difficult to formulate the broad principles that have to be upheld. First, liberalization in the areas of export, import and information technology enabled services must satisfy bilateral interests. Secondly, the contractual decisions for international business operations must be made intrinsically transparent. Thirdly, the State's support to the domestic firms should be free of discrimination. This would, in turn, need a clean government whose members cannot be bribed for securing competitive advantage. A nation must have a well-defined and uniform taxation policy within and an equitable say in the world trade tariffs outside. Only if it is governed well will a nation be able to safeguard its economic interests in the era of globalization.

Conclusion

Globalization spurred by the information technology revolution, has coincided with the emergence of a uni-polar world. This has thrown up new issues of economic security, political sovereignty, and competitiveness at the international market-place. Global economy does not detract from the importance of the national government and the country's corporate world coming closer to each other. The intelligence community is having to enlarge its turf not only to protect the proprietary information in the strategic areas of defence but also for preventing industrial espionage. Economic intelligence, of course, helps to safeguard economic security – particularly by strengthening vigilance against internal sabotage or malpractices. A wider challenge to the intelligence agencies, however, has arisen from the fact that the world has now transited to an era of covert warfare directed against the country's information systems and economic assets. It is only appropriate that international co-operation is growing rapidly to deal with the forces, which are out to unleash terrorism and economic sabotage to pursue their nefarious objectives.

References

1. *Washington Post,* November 5, 1993.
2. '*My FBI*' by Louis J. Freeh, St. Martin's Press, New York, 2005.
3. *Hindustan Times,* New Delhi, February 13, 15, 2006.
4. *Hindustan Times,* New Delhi, September 24, 2005.

6

Studying the Competitor

- **In these times, when stability is no longer the norm, heading a business is no less than leading a combat with the adversaries who may or may not be visible.**

If you think you have no competitor, think again. An enterprise has to know all about the identified competitors in order to devise strategies for gaining a lead. In this endeavour, capital investment alone will not help nor will the mere hiring of highly paid managers. The whole organization has to synergise on the shared goal of making value addition. The firm has to know all about the new entrants in its own sphere of business and the substitute products and services that may be making their appearance. It has to keep track of the bargaining power of the suppliers and buyers. Remember that the existing competitors are all the time driven by rivalry and trying to undercut your market share of business.

A quest for excellence is an assured path for reaching a competitive edge and retaining it too. For this also, a constant inflow of information about competitors and competitive environment becomes necessary so that bench-marks can be established. Study of the competitor has to go along with the assessment of the competitive atmosphere. Among the rivals who are peak performers, there is scope for gaining an exclusive lead through a better insight into what lies ahead. Anticipating actions of the competitors brings in a basic advantage. Business intelligence is all about human thinking and activity going on in the rival camp. Remember, companies do not compete, it is the people in the companies who compete. The key elements in the competition have to be identified and studied. This may enable a player in business to detect an opportunity or visualize a problem in time.

It is legitimate for businesses to get reliable information on the strong points of the rival products and then to enter the market with a superior alternative. Before the Japanese got into the cruise business, they sent their designers to cruises all over the world, to extensively photograph the dining halls, bars, swimming pools and the lounge chairs etc. and ascertain the most popular features there by recording, relative presence of people at each place. It took them several years to make this preparatory effort but this gave them success over the best rivals in that business.

Conducting research on a company is one of the most common competitive intelligence tasks. There are several key areas in which information is required for carrying out such a research. Ascertaining the company's background involves study of its history, image, key executives and advisors, strength of employees in major categories with their salary structures, its profitability and its corporate culture. In this, clues can come from operational information like the progress of the upcoming facilities if any, as also from marketing information that would include market share, clients served and advertising strategies put in place.

Studying the competition means finding out all about the leader of the competing organization. Sometimes the Chairman or the Chief Executive Officer is actively assisted by one or two other influential people in that organization in deciding upon the strategic direction of the firm. It is amazing how much of insight into the working of an organization can be had from an authentic study of the personality profile of its leadership. Things like childhood history and background of education would have greatly determined the psychology and vulnerabilities of the leader under study. He could be a man who is never satisfied enough with the current position of his firm in business and is all the time striving to take new strategic initiatives. His work background will reveal how the person handled situations that arose in his earlier organization and will throw some light on his current attitudes. He may have become conservative in pursuit of the business goal or may have become intrepid enough to be freely driven by instinct. It is also important to know how the person being studied, spends his time and money and what is it that he cares about most deeply in his private life. Collecting all this information would invariably require a combination of facts available in the open and those accessed through the use of special skills for gathering intelligence.

Competitors have to be studied for competitive benchmarking which helps a firm to upgrade its operations. You must profile your rival's management and understand how it will make decisions. You have to cut through your competitor's smoke-screen and accurately read his strategy. Study of the competitors helps to identify sources of critical change in the market and predict significant competitive moves materializing there. A firm must particularly watch out against predators entering the market and pick up early warning signals indicating their arrival.

A business firm is like a living organism. The leadership is its brain, the managers are its limbs and the employees are the body muscles. Studying the competitor therefore means not only a determination of what its leadership is like but also how the entire inside of that organization is performing. Leading companies in the West today take the help of professionals in studying the companies in competition. The information collected ranges from the company's background, its present and upcoming facilities to the salaries of the major group of employees. It is necessary to ascertain the firm's key ownership, the exchange on which its securities are traded and the reputation it enjoys among the customers and in the media. In order to have an idea of the company's profitability, it is important that the fixed costs are delineated from the variable costs. The company's product lines, specifications of products, supply channel, shipping methods as well as marketing and advertising strategies have to be examined. The study would have to take into account information on sales and customer services which would mean finding out the size of its sales force, nature of compensations, and the key sales channels used by it.

Background of the firm's key corporate executives and advisors throws some light on its fortune. The core areas of information are the company's focus on new product development and its market entry strategies. An idea of the intellectual capital of a rival company can be of great help in formulating your own competitive moves. The corporate culture of the firm has to be examined too as also its legal stance and the functioning of the unions among its employees. It goes without saying that this enormous cross-spectrum information on the competition would need an in-depth analysis by knowledgeable people. Their findings would certainly help a firm to take vital strategic decisions for its own advancement. Today, business fortunes are not defined by investment and sale. A monopoly can be easily destroyed even by a smaller player who is innovative about exploiting some facet of the reigning product or service of the competitor. An intelligent firm enjoying a reputation for its home products lasting 'for a life time,' must be following a strategy of creating the need for replacing the gadget over a certain period, without putting this reputation in jeopardy. This is a fine point which the company's rivals must investigate into.

To understand any important competitor, the firm, as already mentioned, has to conduct a comprehensive research. Before embarking on this exercise, it should mop up the in-house knowledge within its own organization available with its own representatives, sales people and other members who may be in a position to unravel some aspects of that competitor. The open sources of information on the rival would include the annual general report and other published accounts of the latter, records of the government, information that your contacts in the industry can give, material available with business analysts, news media and professional data providers. Business interactions and interviews may provide many an insight into the competitor's firm. Help of investigative agencies may be taken and your firm's own intelligence setup may be tasked to gather information confidentially.

A mistake many organizations make about their competitors is to underestimate the latter's capabilities. An organization does not necessarily have to be a leader in its industry to challenge others at the national level. The challenge may come from a particular individual of another firm in the industry who is aggressive, intelligent and dominant. You should know about such a competitor so that you can either try to combat him effectively or find some way of bringing him on to your side. It is prudent to avoid taking on the strengths of the competitor. It is better to take advantage of its weaknesses instead.

A successful strategy has three major ingredients – knowledge about the competition, awareness of the firm's own skills and resources – good, indifferent or poor – and a sensitive insight into the beliefs and values of the people working for the organization. The essence of a successful strategy is to use these ingredients to maximise opportunities for the firm. Some senior managers cannot even name the leaders of the firms competing with them. You have to know the leadership of the rival firm well enough to have an idea of even its psychological makeup. You may otherwise find it so much more difficult to ascertain that firm's strategic objectives. As regards the formulation of your own strategy, it is better if this is done by a team because a collectivity of minds is more likely to make a fail-safe decision. If there is synergy among the team members they will accentuate each other's strength. It is said that in the 1990's, British Airways became the top airline in the world because it had a Chairman in Lord King who concentrated on the vision and a Managing Director in Sir Colin Marshall who was strong in implementation.

Businesses today have to watch out for a new trend of the strong and the able trying to come together to push the weaker players aside. The joint ventures of the weak would not stand unless the constituents have some strengths that so complement each other as to fuse together to create a new business entity capable of standing competition. The future belongs to the companies that evolve out of competitiveness and rely primarily on their internal excellence. The Corporate Executive Board, a research group in Washington, is said to have found, on a study of Fortune 500 companies in the mid 90's, that more than eighty per cent of the causes that marred the growth of a business organization came from the factors of internal functioning. As far as the importance of competitive intelligence is concerned, it is reported that many of these companies employ staff for monitoring competitors.

We must remember that Nature established change as a harbinger of benevolence. The pace of change set by globalization, however, is man-made and not necessarily geared to human welfare per se. The new rules of the game governing the competition will hopefully revert some day to a code that acknowledges the concept of 'the largest good of the largest number' and accept the desirability of the economic uplift of the entire humanity. For this, we need ethical corporations who compete without taking recourse to fraudulent practices and who succeed on the strength of a genuine admiration of their stake-holders.

Conclusion

Reliable information on the strong points as well as the weaknesses of the key players in the competition or the rival products, is the anchor on which you can base your efforts to get the better of them. Best practices have to be studied to establish bench-marks. Capital investment alone cannot guarantee success because a smaller but smarter player who is innovative and aggressive, can beat you to the finish line. Intelligence about the sources of significant competitive moves in the market, helps to pick up early warning signals or, more importantly, to create a new opportunity of gaining an edge or retaining one's monopoly. It makes sense for a player to work on his own strength and the rival's weakness.

7

Competitive Environment

- **It is surprising how most people have little idea of what to do to find out what they need to know.**

A firm exists in a state of uncertainty unless it acquires a complete knowledge of the competitive environment. Study of the variables in the competitive scene is an ongoing process and businesses should be prepared to make suitable investments to keep themselves updated on the external determinants that impact on their progress. It is necessary to know about all that is happening outside the organization in that industry. The market has to be examined and analyzed. Elements in the environment that have a bearing on the firm's interests range from the political dispensation and the tax regime on the one hand to the socio-cultural milieu, demographic features and the technological back-up of the economy, on the other. The enterprise must know all about the trends and expectations in the area of its main services and products.

Businesses would do well to follow a few precepts when engaged in assessing the competitive environment. First, while examining the external situation do not indulge in wishful thinking or merely seek corroboration of what you want to believe. Secondly, establish credibility of the information you receive through some collateral confirmation. Thirdly, the power of domestic competitors even if they are smaller in size must always be carefully evaluated and their sources of advantage identified so that a practical strategy of getting over them can be formulated. Fourthly, the firm must fully exploit the knowledge about the competitors that members of its own organization tacitly carry with them. It may not necessarily be found with the senior management but may be there with the men of the sales department who spend a lot of time in the field. Finally, the facts about the competitive environment have to be examined and analysed in conjunction with the firm's own strengths and weaknesses so that erroneous business decisions are avoided and the right plans put into action.

Study of the market place begins with the examination of the domestic economic factors and the features of the markets abroad. The local markets may be dominated by regional enterprises that have the advantage of commandeering important local skills, enjoying a special hold on the local infrastructure, and drawing strength from their rapport with the local politicians. In the age of technological innovation, no product or service is immune to the threat of substitution. Monopoly profits attract rivals who go all out to get a share of the market for that product. Predators with spare funds meant to buy out businesses for entering a new growth area, exist in the market place all the time. Also, customers may create their own supply service to cut out the current suppliers and the suppliers, likewise, may enter into a new segment of industry abandoning the old customers.

Innovation and change is the maxim in today's world of global competition. Your rival may appear on the scene by proxy from across the seven seas and threaten you with a cheaper product of matching quality. He may choose not to make a profit immediately because he has the strength to balance this temporary investment against profitability that exists for him in another region or country. Such a global player enjoys the inherent advantage of the economy of scale. A firm which does not have business activities worldwide can, however, still compete with the bigger players by constantly improving and innovating at home.

Conducting business on a global basis requires a new frame of mind. Communication technologies have made the markets border-less. A global market-place establishes a new level of competition, a whole new playing field and new rules. Europe's emergence as a single market of over 400 million consumers has affected all businesses around the world. Business operations overseas require a great deal of planning, foresight and knowledge. Intelligence is needed to evaluate the demand and the competition, as also a whole lot of external factors that would impact on that business. A decision to move into a new market should be based on a careful assessment of the opportunities indicated in the new environment.

The scan of the external environment has to cover everything that is capable of affecting the organization's interests. The external factors must be objectively examined for their bearing on the given business. Of prime importance are the five broad features – political, legal, economic, socio-cultural and technological – that basically determine the competitive environment. A company can face potential hardship if it has not adequately analyzed and assessed the political risk while exploring a new market. It is important to analyze the legal system within the target market and its efficacy in controlling the law and order. A company would not like to invest heavily into a market that is not only economically depressed but has been on a downward spiral. An incoming firm will want to feel confident that the market in question has the infrastructure in place to support its business. An intelligent enterprise never overlooks the impact of social and cultural factors on its competitiveness. Demographic changes are an important determinant of the socio-cultural scene. Finally, the technological maturity of the market you enter has to be examined. The level of use of technology has a proportionate influence on business.

For any business enterprise, the study of the political spectrum and the key elements therein is important. The firm must carefully examine if there are political factors that would affect its operations in the country. The study of political dispensation includes ascertaining the methods of political decision-making and the exercise of policy preferences, in operation. Governments are known to have become hostile to certain businesses for political or ideological reasons. A key point of knowledge is to find out if in the structure of governance there are some elements who can exercise a veto on decisions. The firm has to look for shifts in inter-party and intra-party balance and explore in advance the ways and means of getting legitimate access to the right people in the government. An intelligent organization knows that it takes time to build contacts and be in a position to communicate with the political and administrative functionaries exercising regulatory powers. Competitive advantage can be gained if you and not your rivals are aware of an upcoming legislative change or executive order that would affect business.

Sometimes a defined policy framework runs into nuanced interpretations at the cutting edge and the firm would do well to have contacts among the local confidants of the political leaders representing the area, to understand and deal with them. It should also know the people running the local newspapers. In the era of coalition politics, the importance of political forces rooted in the regional appeal has increased. At the local level, there may be politicians who may be backing the domestic competitor and influencers who may be colluding with the local bureaucracies to impede the entry of other players from outside. The state and local political and bureaucratic structures, in any case, have a standing role in running the penal and taxation systems and any business establishment or professional organization located in their jurisdiction must know all about them.

An intelligent firm is aware that third parties can enter the scene as pressure groups anywhere by exploiting local irritants. Even if the firm is global it has to be attuned to this possibility. It has to be vigilant about the prospects of an organized public protest or a strike action developing against any aspect of its operations. The environment lobby today is particularly strong in target identification. A firm that comes out strong in the area of social responsibility in the peacetime will be better placed to deal with its moments of difficulty caused by any third party.

The doctrine of Nobel Laureate Herbert A. Simon that 'a growing number of political constituencies have to acquiesce if a business is to continue its economic mission' largely holds out.[1] The situation is made more complex by three factors. One is the rise of business-politics nexus which damages the level playing field needed for a fair competition. The other is the fragmentation of party system that makes things worse. It has shortened the ruling spans of political leaders with the result that the latter are guided more and more by a tenure-oriented approach and are inclined to make opportunistic decisions for short-run benefits to the neglect of long term costs. Yet another determinant in the political regime is rooted in Vilfredo Pareto's law – 'a few govern the many' which suggests that the elite rules the masses under different political labels and resorts to decision-making processes that are designed to benefit the few at the top, cutting across political divides. An understanding of these inner complexities of the political scenario is necessary for the business enterprises which have to take high-stake strategic decisions.

It would be advisable for the business houses to establish themselves as the representatives of the cause of the common good and demonstrate that while pursuing the mission of profits they stand for the interest of the society. It is good to know that in India some business houses like the Tatas and the Infosys have built a positive reputation in this area. Industry associations and chambers of commerce should try to build a collective influence and voice against political arbitrariness and should be seen to be on the side of the people in building the national economy.

A new enterprise should have an idea of the expectations in the sphere of its main services and products. It should take note of any social trends in the area such as the strong inclination of the people there in favour of a pollution-free atmosphere. Also remember that marketing methodology may be global but consumer's preferences are local in the sense of being culturally influenced. Mass markets have given way to highly segmented ones and this trend has made the information about customers an extremely valuable knowledge. The choices and attitudes of customers are conditioned as much by their purchasing power as by their cultural profile, their belief system and their own awareness of what is happening in the world outside. The cultural patterns of the consumers will shape their responses to a product. Knowing this, global business corporations like the McDonald's and Baskin Robbins offer burgers made from lamb and not beef in India and green tea flavoured ice creams in Japan respectively. When Baskin Robbins entered the Indian market in early Nineties, some of its ice creams contained bone marrow. It took it only a few years to turn completely vegetarian and position this as its USP. Frazer and Haws of London have introduced an expensive lineup of sterling Ganeshas in the Indian market.

Multinational corporations today have to have the ability of managing cultural diversity within the organization and developing suitable strategies for dealing with the cultural profiles in the regions to which the business operations are being extended. The interplay of global integration and the variations in local responsiveness makes the mandate of top managers even more arduous. Handling cross-cultural issues poses a new challenge. It is cultural separation and not geographical distance that the enterprise should take note of. We are in the days of global managers who have the knowledge and sensitivity to respect cultural variants and to put these to good advantage by using the skill of leveraging differences. They know how culture provides the social energy that can be harnessed for driving the outfit. There is increasing realization that global firms have to have managers with a global mind-set. Such a manager has the ability to maintain relationships across geographical expanses and cultural differentials. He realizes that culture determines attitude to work, approach to family and the definition of leisure time. Within the organization, he manages cultural diversity as an asset and utilizes it for enriching the firm's knowledge base and for encouraging newer ideas. Today, a firm should be willing to make some investment, beyond hiring language interpreters, for understanding cultural proclivities of the customers constituting a market.

An important aspect of the study of socio-cultural scene is to find any noticeable demographic trends such as the ageing of the population which may somewhere affect the organization's work force itself or a shift in the patterns of family which may create new demands. Demographic profile has a bearing on the classification of a product in terms of its being a service, a consumption item or an information package. This is also linked with the evaluation of the target groups of consumers based on age, sex, region, profession or income bracket. Changing demography is an important part of social change and this has to be studied to identify the shifts in the consumer's behaviour, attitude and buying habits. Emphasis on the knowledge of socio-cultural profiles underlines the fact that all business relates to human activity and highlights the importance of the human factor in determining whether an enterprise will achieve a competitive edge or not.

Assessing the competitive environment is becoming a huge exercise in information gathering and intelligence analysis. The analysis should be objective and not dictated by what you desire should happen. Some foreign companies operating in Indonesia during the regime of President Suharto were so taken in by the apparent political stability there, that they could not read the signs of revolution that ultimately threw out the dictator in 1978. These companies suffered in the bargain. On the other hand, there is this story about Samsung analysts taking note of an American press report that one of the last guitar factories in the US was closing down due to the less expensive Korean imports and moving in fast to get Samsung to ship all the guitars it could to the US warehouses. The analysis was that guitar was a symbol of national culture of America and that in all probability the US government would step in to protect its domestic product by raising tariff on imports. This is what happened and Samsung made a huge profit on the stockpile.

An event like 9/11 which was bound to produce a huge politico-legal impact on the world was also to create out-of-the-ordinary consequences for business. When the Intelligence Reform and Terrorism Prevention Act of 2004 in the US specifically banned butane lighters from airplanes, Zippo, a leading manufacturer of refillable lighters, lost a share of business. The gainer was the largest match maker of America, D D Bears & Sons which got back some of the market share it had lost earlier to the lighters.[2]

In a scenario where the economy is moving towards globalization, a mismatch can arise between national sovereignty and national economy. An integrated world economy facing a splintered world polity can become a cause for conflicts. The big players in business will have to rise above their monopolistic advantages and think of creating opportunities for the weaker sections of the global society. Managers in future will find it necessary to act as integrators in a pluralistic society and to tackle changes in the social and political order. The business leaders everywhere must start thinking of dealing with the emerging repercussions of globalization. At the macro level, they must keep in mind that globalization will never dilute the importance of a nation as a sovereign player in determining the course of economic development and the fortunes of multinational firms on its territory.

Conclusion

Variations in the key elements of the environment directly affect businesses. Ranging from politico-legal regime to demographic changes, they can easily damage the level playing field and leave a company struggling with its own devices to get over a possible disadvantage. A bolt from the blue like 9/11 impacted businesses globally in terms of the uncertainty it created about the efficacy of the mathematical models of business analysis. At the same time, it sent the stocks soaring for the major companies dealing with the issues of industrial security, particularly the business of promoting bio-metrics for identification and authentication. Firms would do well to improve their image of social responsibility to minimize the chances of pressure groups like the environment lobby, surprising them with protest actions. Assessment of the competitive environment requires a significant effort in information gathering and intelligence analysis.

References

1. Rational Decision Making in Business Organizations, Herbert A. Simon, 1979, AER
2. *Newsweek*, April 25, 2005

8

Competitive Analysis

- **It is the ability to anticipate a change that can convert an implicit threat into a gainful response.**

The knowledge era is making over to the Age of Intelligence as is evident from the fact that truly competitive companies are becoming increasingly sophisticated at collecting and processing information to garner intelligence. Competitive intelligence is the product of knowledge that has been verified, analyzed and applied to your business for making a futuristic decision. Today a firm has to have the ability to know when to stop gathering data and move on to analysis. While it is impossible to ignore information, it is very easy to be overwhelmed by it.

Competitive Intelligence is organized, structured information gathering, analysis and processing to enhance strategic decision-making. It is used by businesses to gain a competitive edge by reaching the correct findings about suppliers, customers, regulators and the competitors. Research and analysis process is the most crucial part of any competitive intelligence project. It needs professional skills and rests on a set of well defined concepts. The facts at hand should be credible – uncontaminated by 'misinformation' and the analysis itself should be free of subjective opinion or wishful thinking. The objective of analysis is to enhance the firm's leverage and detect a new opportunity or an emerging problem. Insufficient examination under pressure from any quarter can affect the findings. Any tendency to cover up for inadequacy of facts by making generalizations will not help and it might be prudent therefore to seek further information to fill the gaps in knowledge.

A good intelligence analysis should indicate the best strategy options. The results of competitive analysis should be promptly shared with the decision-makers. There are many ways in which this can be done – written reports, verbal briefing and video presentation, to name a few. The timing of delivery is an essential determinant of the value of intelligence. Remember, the basic strength of the competitive intelligence is that it allows you to act before rather than react to events that can impact on your company or organization.

Analysis for competitive intelligence requires human, financial, databank and technological resources. There are many analysis techniques and more are being developed all the time. The scope of analysis is vast indeed. There are different elements of environment to be analyzed. There is market analysis, industry analysis and analysis of a rival company as well as an occasion to carry out the individual competitor's profile workout. Intelligence analysis, therefore, plays its part at different levels and in different areas of business.

Analysis is the bedrock of competitive bench-marking. Bench-marking is the ongoing process of finding, researching and analyzing best-in-class organizations, products, services, business operations and management practices which will lead to improvement within one's own enterprise. Bench-marking means learning from other people's mistakes and even better, their successes. Effective use of competitive bench-marking techniques helps companies to leap over the competition, avoid costly mistakes and learn from the experiences of other organizations. Since change is the one constant in business today, bench-marking works well as an on-going process. Since industry methods continually change, bench-marking analysis becomes the means of ensuring continuous improvement. To make one's organization innovative and help it to keep up its vision, one has to track and evaluate the advances in technology so that those that are worthwhile would be adopted. Firms which make bench-marking a part of the strategy formulation, have to invest appropriately on a comprehensive competitor analysis workout. Such firms have an opportunity of becoming great allies in the bench-marking process and achieving strategic partnerships on the strength of their complementary best-in-class record in specific operational areas.

There are a number of factors to analyze when you are determining the potential or opportunity within a new market. The scan of the environment should include, apart from the industry-specific information, an analysis of political, legal, economic, socio-cultural and technological factors. A company can run into road-blocks if it does not adequately analyze and assess the political risks while exploring a new market. It is also important to analyze the legal system within the target market. A company would not like to invest heavily into a market that has been on a downward spiral economically with no hopeful features. A related matter is whether the market has the infrastructure in place to support your line of business. It is vital that you approach any competitive intelligence project that involves contact with international sources, with a sensitivity to the culture you are entering. Understanding the cultural diversity of the new place is necessary for evaluating behaviors, attitudes and buying habits. Last but not the least, the technological maturity of the market you enter must be analyzed before you launch your business project there.

Competent analysis produces intelligence in the form of readings on the likely changes in the market place, any emerging class of consumers, the possible moves of a competitor, identifiable acquisition targets, and impending regulatory changes that could affect your business. Success and failures of others could be analyzed as case studies so that one could learn from them. The objective of the case study is to identify the problem and to define the right strategic option to deal with it. Such an analysis should be attempted only after securing the right information. Competitive analysis gives a firm better insight and early warning signals which enable it to gain an edge over the rivals. The analysts have to look across the entire commercial horizon for competitive danger and screen the entire business environment particularly for spotting new entrants. A large number of global companies have established competitive intelligence and analysis departments. The Swedish company ABB has a huge wing for this under the umbrella of the planning department and it is answerable to the CEO. This wing even trains managers in intelligence. The Swedes see competitive intelligence as a non-military way of safeguarding their political and economic security.

An intelligent firm should be willing to allocate funds for the resources that are needed for competitive analysis. Human resources are required along with the skills of library, internet, and database research, the ability to conduct interviews for culling out information, and the training to sift facts for market analysis. Financial resources would be needed for commissioning studies, buying directories and acquiring membership of beneficial associations. Technological resources like internet access, data-warehouse software and software for data mining are extremely important. It costs money to get hold of informational resources like the annual reports of the competitors, reports published by the government and the publications of trade or industry conglomerates. What the firms often ignore is the importance of their own knowledge inventory that has to be kept ready for the analysts. The company must maintain a detailed record of where knowledge resides within the organization, what contacts and secondary sources of information do the firm's own staff have and what other skills of information-gathering do the insiders possess to the company's advantage. Intelligence analysis must have the maximum support of all potential information producers in the firm. Data gathering and analysis of information to produce intelligence should roughly take a similar share of the project time.

Competitive analysis must conform to the following seven point code : First, it should be focused on keeping up the firm's leverage and detecting a new opportunity or an emerging problem. Second, the analyst must establish the credibility of information before accepting it. Third, the analysis and projection should arise out of the facts analyzed. Injection of bias or wishful thinking can lead to failures. Fourth, analysis should not be marred by insufficient examination under pressure for time or any other contingency. Fifth, the analyst should not resort to generalizations to cover up for the inadequacy of data. He should clearly state the gaps in information that have been noticed. Sixth, it is a cardinal sin for the analysts to tailor the readings to please the masters. Lastly, the analysis must indicate the best strategy options. If the facts and analysis are uncontaminated, the course of action would tend to suggest itself.

Conclusion

Competitive intelligence is, in a large measure, the product of an incisive analysis of the information gathered in a structured way. The outcome of analysis can be marred by insufficient examination, inadequacy of facts, or lack of objectivity. Competent analysis should yield readings on the competitors and the competitive environment that can help the firm to plan its own operations. Businesses need to take intelligence-based decisions and they should not be pennywise about spending on the resources that are required to produce business intelligence through analysis. Potential within a new market, bench-marking for ensuring continuos improvement, evaluation of risks, assessment of technological factors, and identification of acquisition targets, are the crucial areas where analysis helps a firm to come to the right decisions. Professional analysis is becoming the most important aid for businesses for choosing their strategy options.

9

Knowledge Creation

- **We often see things without observing them, observe without absorbing them and absorb without comprehending what is significant or out-of-the-ordinary about them.**

The difference between a man and an animal is that the former has a sense of information. He has the capacity to retain knowledge and an ability to use recall before choosing a course of action. The man has a range of emotions, all of which are triggered by information. A complete man is an information conscious man who can connect pieces of facts and read new meanings in them. He senses gaps in information and fills them up by seeking additional inputs. Information pulls him out of illusions and myth. It gives him strength to take calculated risks as his responses are seasoned by knowledge. An information savvy man gets the best results for his effort.

Man is gifted with the spirit of inquiry and it is his quest for answers that creates knowledge. Knowledge is preserved and multiplied through communication of information as the oral tradition of early societies proved so well. The dialogue of the sages or thinking men gave the human society knowledge of how nature works and what governs the consequences of human action. In our times, the new information technology has created new measurement tools, new forms of databases and new mathematical models to create knowledge.

Knowledge is evolutionary because it can only take you forward. What is known cannot become unknown but it can be superceded by new information. Knowledge is, therefore, the new weapon of competition in our times. In industry and business, success comes to the companies that have the best information and know how to use it most effectively and not necessarily to the firms that have the most financial muscle. Information is the new raw material which leads to new products, services and marketing strategies. IBM gets more revenues from selling computer services than from selling computers. Information helps a business to do something faster, better or cheaper. Japanese manufacturers made a huge gain by substituting information for inventory. They dispensed with stockpiles by ensuring that parts were delivered just in time. In the new era, wealth is the product of knowledge. That is why a firm today must protect its intellectual capital which includes the intelligible knowledge of its work force. This can give it a competitive edge.

The knowledge resource that a business organization can develop to its competitive advantage includes, in a major sense, the totality of tacit understanding that the work force of the firm has, of the merits and demerits of the products and processes handled by the enterprise. To locate and pool in this subterranean knowledge has become a prime function of the management science today. Laying down channels of interaction and facilitating communication are among the principal tasks of the top management anywhere. Knowledge management has become an inseparable part of strategic planning in business.

No business organization can be considered to be knowledgeable if it only looked for information that is available outside and did not garner the substantial amount of knowledge that lies buried within that organization in its documents or exists in the minds of the members of that corporate body. An intelligent organization, in order to stay competitive, must ensure that knowledge of individual members is not only tapped but also put together as a resource that is used for the exposition of new thoughts and themes. The important thing is to establish a tradition by which the members connect their ideas to those of others. Holding occasional brain-storming sessions is not enough; what is needed is an atmosphere that facilitates inter-personal communication and exchange of ideas that strike the work force during its hands-on spells. Innovative thoughts on new products and processes are born in such an ambience. The history of business is replete with examples of how firms gained a competitive edge through this process. Knowledge creation needs removal of hierarchical insulation within the organization, participative discussions across the functional boundaries subject to the requirement of restrictive security, and a well-established system of credit sharing. Identifying a problem is a good outcome in terms of knowledge creation. Right questions unearth a snag, a challenge or a gap and lead to a new solution or innovation. It is for the top leadership of the firm to ensure that information is treated as an orgnizational resource.

An intelligent enterprise knows how to unlock the hidden assets it has in the form of the untapped knowledge that exists by way of the unrevealed talent of its employees, the thinking of its customers, and the collective pluses and minuses of its systems and procedures. This is the intellectual capital that can help to make the operations cost-effective and hence more profitable. Rise of the knowledge worker is leading to new principles of managing people. Employees are today, the most important asset of any organization. The concept of a collective labour force is yielding to the idea of every individual becoming a distinct production source. The knowledge worker uses his thinking brain and not merely his hands while at work. He adapts more quickly to a changed process because he understands change and probably is the initiator of that change himself. He is the sheet anchor of business in these times when stability is no longer the norm. The information revolution has reinvented business and society. Knowledge has become the primary ingredient of what we make, do, buy or sell. Today, building intellectual capital and making the best use of it has become the most important task of both business enterprises as well as the nations at large. Even for military strategists there are new dimensions of war as, in future, wars would be fought outside the battle fields in the unseen realm of information systems. There is no industry or company today that has not become more information-intensive and dependent on knowledge as a major determinant of all activity and operations.

An intelligent enterprise understands three basic concepts about the handling of its knowledge resource. First, it accepts that forecasting or anticipating business trends is not so much a matter of luck as a logical putting together of information garnered from within and outside the organization. It acknowledges the reality that crucial bits and pieces of information may be lying scattered and that if brought together for collation and analysis they could provide the larger picture containing a valuable indicator for the future. Secondly, the business leaders should have a look at the total information available and avoid falling into the human weakness of accepting only that which seems plausible, to the disregard of whatever looked out of the ordinary. Many managers disown information just because it does not fit in with the known pattern. They run the risk of missing out on something that could truly be path-breaking. Lastly, the strategic planning division of the firm is the correct slot where knowledge creation function should be housed. This task has to be overseen by the firm's apex because it is here that the vision and mission of the enterprise is defined.

Sometimes inability to accept change leads to serious strategic blunders. The typewriter companies presumed that personal computers were too heavy to carry and became oblivious to the movement of technology towards miniaturization. The advent of electronic notebook gave them a sudden setback. They had not paid enough attention to the work going on in the connected fields. In the age of information, knowledge comes in integral packages which means that the degree of completeness of knowledge in one sphere depends on the access to information in other spheres that are connected with it. A teacher for instance who handles children will be considered better than others if she has knowledge of child psychology as well. Today an employer has to be aware of the laws pertaining to the so-called sexual harassment at the place of work.

Since public knowledge is shared by everybody, its utilization for competitive advantage depends on the firm's ability to churn it for innovation. It is here that the in-house knowledge of the enterprise becomes very important. Japanese automobile industry is said to have this intrinsic advantage flowing from an efficient system of utilization of internal knowledge. The top leadership overseeing the knowledge management must naturally create an atmosphere in which information assets of the firm will be kept well guarded by every member. The entire discipline and trade craft of business vigilance and corporate security must be brought into full play. A well nursed corporate culture bolsters this defence by attaching special value to corporate loyalty.

The business world has a lot to learn from an intelligence organisation in the vital area of managing change. In the information age where organizations or in fact, whole societies are being transformed, the basic requisite of leadership is the ability to create and guide the process of change. An intelligence organization is fully attuned to the challenge of change because its agenda can shift in accordance with the change in the profile of the adversary. At no level in the organization does the manager or the operator face the same situation twice. The autonomous function of initiating a move is therefore built into the working of all members regardless of their placing in the hierarchy. A business enterprise today is also in need of employees who can initiate a move. This calls for a suitable change in the managerial practices that stood for the status quo. Primacy of 'control' has to give way to participative supervision and shared initiatives. The leadership of an 'intelligent' firm understands that information revolution has generally reduced the life span of strategic plans and made management of brand and market share much more difficult.

The success of any organization depends on how well its members adapt their individual strengths to work together.

By discarding the traditional command and control style of management in favour of one that encourages good working relationships among the employees, the leaders in management can expect to reach creative and productive business solutions. The test of an intelligent organization is that it understands and implements the concept that 'productivity of a group is larger than the sum of the individual productivities.' It wants its leaders to nurture the development of others at all levels of the organization so that success would be sustained in future when they are not around. All people have an untapped leadership potential which can be developed with experience. In the information age, the prime quality of leadership is the ability to take knowledge based decisions. Today's leaders are therefore both born and made.

A gifted birth or a high IQ will not guarantee success unless the attitude is right. Attitude determines how one would act. Luckily one can retrain one's attitude by making attitude a matter of choice. By learning to accept that there is a higher perspective in any situation one can achieve a healthy stability of response in the face of the changing environment. In an intelligent organization, the management emphasizes the winning combination of mental application and freedom from fear of failure, to achieve time bound production. This is a matter of inculcating the right attitude and motivation in the work force. Remember, fear of failure can cause cessation of learning.

Management of knowledge is for creating new insights. In the age of knowledge it is the peeps into the future that will create and sustain competitive advantage. Most managers remain preoccupied with identifying the current sources of advantage in relation to the company and the industry of which it is a part. Thinking into the future does not come easy. It feels safe to deal with what is immediate and at hand.

Quest for the unseen generates fears of the unknown. Knowledge creation would however be worthwhile only if it guides advancement into the future—into the area of intelligent anticipation.

Knowledge generation should additionally be geared to tracking the current and the likely new competitors and their strategies, looking out for the arrival of new products, monitoring the changes in the competitive environ covering the legal, socio-political and demographic shifts as well as the developments on the technology front, and finally to identifying, quantifying and securing the firm's exclusive knowledge against the prying attempts of the adversaries. A progressive firm lays down the structural and operational mechanisms for knowledge generation and conversion of knowledge into competitive intelligence. Toshiba is reported to have established an Advanced Information, Intelligence and Integration Division manned by analysts who are capable of constructing concepts that can be projected for the company's advancement. A strategic business decision is not uni-dimensional as the business analysis on which it rests has to take into account the impact of an innovation on the consumers, prospects of substitution attempts by competitors, stability of its value in the future, the need for an advertisement campaign and finally the firm's commitment to corporate ethics. The information road map in business has three segments – knowledge generation, intelligence analysis and formulation of strategy. These correspond to the stages of 'production,' 'assessment,' and 'action' known to an intelligence organisation.

The success of those who handle human resource development should be judged by the progress they achieve in establishing an atmosphere where innovative thinking is encouraged and every member shares knowledge with others in the organization without fear of criticism or skepticism about recognition and rewards. Generation of knowledge and its sharing within the enterprise should become an index of loyalty and personal identification with the company's vision. The top management would do well to establish a tradition of periodical audit through appropriate procedures, of the various aspects of knowledge generation and organizational learning in the context of the firm's activities and plans. Competitive intelligence in the age of globalization can lead to major transformations in business, both in its organizational structures as well as its corporate goals. It can compel mergers, joint ventures and termination of product portfolios.

The age of knowledge has transformed the concept of work force from a mass of semi-skilled staff to an assembly of individual performers who can make value addition to the business operations by creating new learning. Logically therefore, the system of selection, the programmes for in-house competence building and other strategies of human resource development, acquire a new meaning. The company needs to make investments on staff—financial, emotional and nurtural—if it wants to raise committed knowledge workers.

Conclusion

It is the spirit of inquiry that triggers the man's quest for answers and generates knowledge. Knowledge is preserved when it is communicated without flaws. Knowledge today is the base of all business strategies, a telling example of which is the use of information by some manufacturers for ensuring that part were delivered just in time to eliminate the need for stockpiles and inventory. The intelligible knowledge of the work force, waiting to be harvested as the intellectual capital of the firm, is a crucial organizational resource which the top leadership of the enterprise must not fail to secure. This may yield innovative ideas leading to new products, services and value addition, giving the firm a competitive edge. An employee today has to be treated as a knowledge worker and as a distinct production source because he applies his thinking – not merely his hands – while at work. If handled properly, he can prove to be the initiator of change to the advantage of the enterprise. Managerial practices, unfortunately, have not moved fast enough in the direction of establishing an atmosphere within the firm that would encourage innovative thinking.

10

An 'Intelligent' Home

- **Distinguishing essentials from non-essentials is measure of rare competence.**

Intelligence, basically, is information on the basis of wh. you take a decision on a matter that has futuristic implicatioı There are situations both in private and professional spher where before opting for a course of action, one would l required to evaluate the present, recall its connectivities wit the past, and try to foresee what lies ahead. These are th moments that will either open up the pathway to your goa or land you at a road-block. We live in times when informatioı and foresight are crucial to growth and success.

Today, you have to know your strengths and weaknesses in relation to other players for being able to assess the opportunities or the threats that you could run into. Knowledge gives you control over your present and confidence about your future. It is this element of 'control' that explains why, in the intelligence parlance, it is believed that 'knowledge is power.' To the extent a home is also an 'intelligent' establishment that prepares its young for the future, it should endeavour to facilitate knowledge updating, enhance awareness of the environ, and promote inter-personal co-operation for the common good of that family unit.

The products of an 'intelligent' home are optimistic, intrepid, and diligent. They focus on their objectives, know the difference between self-esteem and ego, and practice rectitude amidst temptations of a none-too-moral social environment. A word on self-esteem and ego deserves a mention here. Self-esteem is a quiet awareness of your worth; ego is a loud presumption of your value. In any interaction with others, self-esteem is a source of positive currents while ego generates negativity. Self-esteem, therefore, can become an instrument of success while ego causes failure. Self-esteem is founded in your conviction that you are equal to the task in hand and in your belief that your choices are moral. Ego is rooted in an ingrained fear of being found unequal to the task and in a lack of commitment to means over ends. Self-esteem creates in you a readiness to give credit to others where due while ego generates in you a desire to get credit over others at any cost. Members of an intelligent organization learn to make these distinctions. Remember, only when you separate your thinking from your ego will you notice your strengths and weaknesses and be able to evaluate them objectively.

Most young parents have got their strategic thinking right with regard to health, education, and the right attitudinal orientation as the priorities for their growing child. They are willing to invest whatever they can in this direction. In a striking demonstration of the tenacity of the parent in safeguarding the future of the child, a mother in a poor Indian hamlet calls her child *'raja beta'* (prince) or *'rani bitiya'* (princess) and promises them all the goodies that their *'Chanda Mama'* (Moon—the celestial uncle) will bring them one day. In a display of supreme intelligence, she helps her child to transcend the consciousness of poverty to grow up without a self-debilitating complex. She does her best to prepare her child for the competitive environment outside the home.

Most homes practice, perhaps unwittingly, a doctrine of intelligence that emphasizes the higher importance of brain over brawn or of skills over physical strength. A classical intelligence organisation, it may be mentioned, attaches great value to the individual's personal resourcefulness and uses it to enhance the competitive advantage of the outfit. An intelligent home also encourages the young to rediscover their own talents and strong points. Further, it tries to define the correctness of means that its young should adopt in pursuing their goals. It is at such a home that the first lessons on how not to sacrifice the long range objective for some short term advantage, are given.

It is, however, a matter of concern that many homes are not living up to the conduct of an 'intelligent' unit and are either allowing the young to be corrupted by the money they have not earned or are letting them take to muscle power in search of influence and material gain. Such youngsters brought up on the distorted perversions of reality would ultimately weaken themselves in the competitive world and possibly drift on to the path of delinquency. The redeeming feature is that the average home, by and large, is still an 'intelligent' organization that prepares its members for banking on their own abilities and skills and not on borrowed strength.

In a classical intelligence organization, the head is a patriarch on whom lies the ultimate accountability for all successes and failures. He exercises participative supervision rather than a despotic control on the establishment, runs the outfit on the principle of optimal utilization of resources, and provides an environment of learning and growth to its members. He promotes the feeling that success of the individual is the success of the entire organization. These are the management objectives that are so truthfully practiced in an intelligent home by the head of the family unit.

Today's successful home is a centre of knowledge where significant trends in all spheres of life are observed and absorbed. An intelligent home should foster the skills of observation, absorption and analysis. It should be its own 'eyes and ears.' Intelligent people are trusting but not credulous and they realize that knowledge helps you to save yourself from unpleasant surprises. An intelligent home trains its members to get attuned to accepting only reliable facts and remembering the disadvantage that can come from a blind acceptance of any information. It makes it possible for them to avert running into an adverse environment because they have the ability to perceive and evaluate sources of hostility in real time and take steps to suitably defuse or neutralize them. Such a home also inculcates an understanding of the importance of retaining a reasonable sense of confidentiality about one's plans for the future. All these are traits of intelligence that are getting rooted in a 'home.' This is a welcome trend.

Good observation is the base of intelligence. We often see things without observing them, observe without absorbing them and absorb without comprehending what is significant or out of the ordinary about them. The famed Sherlock Holmes, immortalized by Sir Arthur Conan Doyle, is not a detective so much as a man of intelligence who succeeds because of his extraordinary power of observation. He translates what he sees into deductions that an ordinary man would not be able to make. In 'The Adventure of the Speckled Band,' Sherlock Holmes tells the unknown girl Helen Stoner who had come to him in a state of acute alarm and fright, that she should not worry any more as she had already stressed herself by driving in a dog-cart along heavy roads before catching the morning train to reach him. The girl bewildered by this accurate description is then told by the detective that there was no mystery about it. Holmes says – 'the left arm of your jacket is spattered with mud in no less than seven places. The marks are perfectly fresh. There is no vehicle save a dog-cart which throws up mud in that way and then only when you sit on the left hand side of the driver.' Holmes had also noted the second half of a return ticket in the palm of the girl's left glove. A watchful man is more likely to get the right information for decision-making. Observation and a spirit of inquiry go together. The curiosity of a child should be considered a good sign and handled with patience and a positive response.

Intelligence is not statistics about inanimate things ; it is information about human interactions, thinking and motivations. It is an ongoing monitoring of the behaviour of the adversary or the competitor and the scanning of the radar screen to detect an opportunity or a threat. Just as the nation's intelligence outfit works for protecting the collectivity of the people constituting that nation, against external threats or internal conflicts, the intelligent home seeks secure existence of its members against inflictions that can come from outside and the injuries that can be caused from within. The parents at such a home provide their children with love and emotional support but they also try to determine the individual's vulnerabilities and strong points so that they can meaningfully help the young to step out into the open on a note of preparedness for the positive and negative elements of the competitive environment.

It is incumbent on those who guide an 'intelligent' home to be keenly aware of the socio-cultural milieu around them, the politico-legal regimen that decides the level of protection offered to an individual by the State, and the economic forces operating outside. The basic skills of observation and deduction mentioned earlier are extremely relevant to a successful assessment of what is happening around. Knowledge of the patterns of crime in the neighborhood, for instance, is important. It may be prudent to advise the children not to take lift in a car if the area is known to be frequented by car-borne criminals. Today, a general awareness that terrorists target innocent civilians congregating for socio-religious activity, has become a necessity. Since it is the human malcontent that is the biggest source of threat to any society, the products of an intelligent home are prepared to test the human turf outside – in office, in the shopping plaza or at the place of entertainment, keeping this in view. They should remember that all planned inflictions originate from human minds.

It could be said that taking a risk is healthy but being unaware of risks is certainly unpardonable. It can lead to a disaster for the individual and for the unit as a whole. The electronic media today draws the young to a world of fiction in the name of entertainment. Fantasies are in order but they should not convert the facts of life into a make-believe. In this context, an intelligent home grants freedom not permissiveness. It knows that today aloofness does not guarantee safety and that one's protection lies in one's ability to make knowledge-based responses. The world is becoming more and more competitive and awareness of what the other side has or does not have helps to bring in some advantage. In an intelligent home, members are information savvy and this is what keeps them from being taken in for a ride easily.

An understanding of human behaviour and a logical bent of mind are said to be the prime requisites for any successful member of a classical intelligence organization. These precisely are the qualities that are needed anywhere else too, for making a success of personal and professional life. An 'intelligent' home may not have any identifiable adversary but it nonetheless imparts an intelligence orientation to its members for their general good. Blind friendships with persons about whose antecedents you have no idea at all, is not in vogue in 'intelligent' homes. Even selfless friendships have to be made with deserving people.

Remember, intelligence has its rightful place even in the arena of emotions. In Tulsi's *Ramacharitmanas,* Hanuman – admittedly renowned for his skills of intelligence – watches Sita in her solitary confinement passing into a state of acute pessimism and depression after an oppressive visit of Ravana to the Asoka Vatika. Instead of suddenly appearing before her as a stranger, Hanuman first lifts her out of her gloom by tossing the ring of Lord Ram in front of her. She recognizes the ring but is vexed by the negative thought wondering who could possibly have vanquished Ram? Hanuman then quickly removes the ambiguity by reciting, while still in hiding, the story of how Ram was already in active pursuit of Sita's trail. He appears before Sita only after turning around her psyche and filling her with optimism. The creator of *Ramacharitmanas* who sketches this portrayal, lived not too far back in history.

Life is becoming more complex everyday. You step out of home and you cannot avert running into people. Whether you want it or not, you have to handle strangers as frequently as those known to you. You have to tackle your own moods on one hand and be alert, on the other, about what is happening in the mind of the person you are interacting with. You have to correctly get at what the other person is trying to put across and at the same time see that you are also not misunderstood. The cause and effect directing the human mind is not easy to fathom because the relationship between the two is not simple any more. Meaningful results come out of interpersonal interactions only if the concerned persons are on the same mental grid during the period of contact. Japanese businesses follow the tradition of not talking shop unless a fairly prolonged inter-mixing at personal level has preceded the actual negotiations.

An intelligent home provides love and care and fulfilment of the emotional needs of its members but it also prepares them for the rough and tumble of the highly interactive life that they would be exposed to. They have to grow up to handle on one hand, all the residual impact of the global vicissitudes and to confront, on the other, the social ills plaguing their immediate environment. Foundations of self-confidence are laid in the formative years of a person. Confidence gets marred in children who are subjected to 'power game' by their parents in an attempt to compel compliance. No child should be over-ruled without being first told why his demand could not be met. Moreover, the child should be made competitive not necessarily combative. The child should be compared with others to emphasize the positive aspects of his personality and not to bring out his inadequacies. Very often the opposite of this is done which dampens the child's belief in his own self. In some homes he gets support of a wrong kind which makes him a bully. The role of early grooming is acknowledged as a significant contributor to the personality of a business leader. Professionals who carry out studies on competitors do try to examine the childhood history of the target. They want to know where the person was born, what was the economic condition in which he or she was placed as a child and what traits the parents might have imparted to him or her.

Midas touch is often acclaimed as a high tribute to a man of commerce and business in the positive sense of his being a role model for entrepreneurship. The tale of Midas, however, is meant to be a warning against greed. Greed is the craving for an undeserved gain. The trouble about a weakness like greed is that it has no limits. Look at the number of chief executives and managing directors of large industrial and business concerns in the world that have in recent times, been exposed for acts of fraud and cheating. Some of them were among the highest paid executives in the world. It is a sobering thought that Midas suffered a most frightening curse because his greed landed him in a position where he turned everything into gold including his young son as well. An intelligent home encourages its members to be pro-active in their quest for legitimate money but keeps them from that debilitating malady called greed.

An intelligent home trains its young through counselling and tasking. Its members can mesh in the lessons of the past in the experience of the present and use both to focus on the future. Such a home values whatever good is seen around. It praises legitimate earning, appreciates the quality of helping the needy, and emphasizes steadfastness in a situation of adversity. An Indian home has the additional merit of being able to supplement the 'Intelligence Quotient' with emotional and spiritual intelligence too. The cultural tradition of India always commended an honest striving for money as not only a matter of right but also as a duty of every citizen. It laid stress on spending or investing money wisely. A rich man enjoyed high social status because he was deemed to have shown virtues of a successful man. He brought to bear on his endeavours qualities of intelligence, diligence and decision-making. Implicit in this was a recognition of the fact that it is not easy to establish and run a successful business enterprise. An intelligent home inculcates this thought process and value system. Today, unfortunately, a person who strikes it rich may be viewed as being successful but not necessarily acknowledged as a decent or respectable individual. This is because the socio-political environment is fuelling the vicious trend where money has got de-linked from the moral code. Among its many consequences is the rising juvenile delinquency rooted in the ill-gotten money passed on to the younger generations.

An intelligent home establishes the bench-mark of fusion between training and development. Home is the only place where there is an assured and uninterrupted growth of the totally uninitiated. It is the only outfit that welcomes an entrant without setting any norms whatsoever, for 'admission.' This is the place where training is regarded as a pleasant responsibility, a self-less gift of the more experienced to the new entrant. The aim of the training is growth. An intelligent home therefore celebrates progress. The whole outfit rejoices if the youngsters happen to surpass the 'trainers' in performance. This is an attitude not easy to find amongst conventional trainers. The head of a family is one 'Chief' who is happy to be left behind on the graph of progress by his trainees in his own lifetime.

In the highly stressful world of today, it is important for an intelligent organization to have a nurturing leadership. Nearly half the working people suffer from work related depression because they perceive insecurity. In a classical intelligence organization, what gives stability to a member is the well-established axiom that the strength of the organization is the strength of the individual and vice-versa. An intelligent home lives up to this precept. It is a unit whose achievements exceed the sum total of the progress made by its individual members. This happens because everybody is left relatively free of any fear of failure which, in turn, enhances his or her output.

We live in a world of exaggerated claims, misinformation, and subtle fraud and to deal with them one needs a mix of shrewdness, pragmatism and awareness of the competitive externalities. Shrewdness is the ability to use intelligence for securing a benefit without causing hurt to someone else. Pragmatism is not a compromise with principles or ethics but a healthy option of examining the feasibility of an approach before pushing ahead with it. Awareness of what others are up to and what has given rise to a certain situation is of course basic to applied intelligence. All these add to the professional foundation on which a classical intelligence organization functions and as precepts they should be followed by an 'intelligent' home too.

Conclusion

A home that shapes the future of its young, has many features of an 'intelligent' establishment. It facilitates acquisition of knowledge, creates awareness of the environ, and grooms its products for handling human relations. It prepares the young for the competitive world by filling him or her with optimism, willingness to work, and a belief in the ethical approach. One of the most remarkable 'management' objectives that an 'intelligent' home puts into practice is to promote the feeling that success of the individual is the success of the entire organization. Such a home is the role model of human resource development through training because it guarantees uninterrupted growth of the totally uninitiated. It indeed establishes a bench-mark in making training a selfless gift of the more experienced to the new entrant and generally providing a nurturing leadership.

11

A Business Leader

- **The learning never ends because the challenge never ceases.**

There are three reasons why businesses today need leaders and not just managers. First of all, an enterprise in these times is constantly exposed to the challenge of change and its responses to the fragile competitive environment go beyond the concern for stability that managers are typically attuned to. Secondly, a firm on a global playing field is a vast organization which needs a thinking head to give it an overall vision and direction. It is no good that the human resource development, the technical wing or the marketing division claims good performance all for itself. The whole corporate body is one organization and an ailment of one part is enough to make the business sick. The head has to be a patriarch to keep the firm in shape and a patriarch is always a leader. Thirdly, globalization is producing a new kind of interface of the firm with the political, economic and technological worlds because of which taking major business decisions is becoming a leadership function and not merely the outcome of a managerial performance. Remember, all leaders can manage but all managers cannot lead.

In the age of information leadership has five essential planks which can be mnemonically abbreviated as DRINK[1]. A leader is a *decision-maker.* His hallmark is *reliability.* He is a person of *initiative* because being pro-active is built into his role. Having initiative or being pro-active is a pre requisite for leading the change. The forces of 'status-quoism' and inertia are strong in any big organization and only the firm's leadership can overcome them. The leader has to have *nerves* because he will be tested by a challenge that calls for grit and not muscle power. Finally, unlike in the past his responses have to be *knowledge-based* so that he moves with awareness of risks and not in ignorance of them. Quite remarkably, these precisely are the attributes of the leader of a modern intelligence organization which only proves that a business enterprise today has to be an 'intelligent' establishment too.

Just as a text has a theme, an analysis has an implied conclusion, and a good diet has some unseen ingredients, the core elements of knowledge are always hidden in the visible bulk of information that is there on any given subject or area. Intelligence is the applied wisdom that provides the ability to sift the important from the unimportant. Leadership rests on this ability. Without it a sound decision cannot be taken. This is a rare gift considering how common it is to see people getting bogged down in details. Bhagwad Gita, read across the national boundaries has Lord Krishna counselling Arjuna on how to take the right decision. The discourse highlights the importance of a mind that is unclogged by emotion, is free of ambiguities, and is imbued with the stability of the larger vision. Without intelligence you cannot discriminate between the essentials and the non-essentials. Also, 'for the uncontrolled there is no intelligence.'[2] A leader follows the simple recipe of macro-vision while taking decisions. He has the spiritual intelligence that becomes necessary if one wants to look at things from a higher plane.

It is only from the sky that you can see the great reality that the earth is round. A broader view adds completeness to your assessment of what you are able to see. It enhances comprehension and reveals the total picture where you can read new meanings in its parts. It discovers unseen connectivities behind events and their consequences. The capacity to take an overview of things is not easily acquired. It is a gift to those who have intelligence tempered with spiritual maturity. It helps a leader to formulate the right integral response. Chanakya points out that 'what is not possible by deployment of force is possible by the use of stratagem.'[3] A business leader who has to operate in combative competitiveness understands the importance of this precept. Successful business leaders strategize by integrating their human resources, the organizational behaviour of their firms, and the developments within and around their businesses. They establish a tradition of decisions being taken not just for demonstrating that there is action but for meeting a business need or purpose.

To act or not to act is a crucial question that crops up ever so often in our lives and we end up either acting on inadequate examination of the situation or prevaricating till the time for action that would give us the best results, is over. Action lacks merit when it is taken without any thinking or is guided by fear or compulsion. Inaction results from inborn procrastination, concern for failure, or lack of awareness. A business leader is able to act on intuition, which is nothing but intelligence uncorrupted by misgivings and doubts. He makes up his mind quickly which is not the same thing as taking a hasty decision. Good business decisions are always a product of three essential ingredients – completeness of information, a healthy awareness of the risks, and a well thought-out plan of implementation.

Having nerves means being intrepid and being intrepid is at the root of confidence. In the age of information, confidence is materially strengthened by knowledge and if knowledge is in the form of intelligence, it gives you foresight and control of circumstances.

A business leader keeps pushing because leadership does not exist in a situation of no action. Action for him is an engagement in the line of duty or '*dharma*'. You cannot be a leader if you are not a doer. Devilish actions are for the demons and since business enterprises are a human endeavour, an ethical framework and value system becomes relevant for them. A business decision is a good decision for the enterprise if it does not create a disconnect with the general good.

A business leader like the patriarch in a family has an extraordinary awareness of his accountability and a total commitment to the advancement of his organization. He runs his establishment on the dual concept of operational freedom for its members and a clearly acknowledged centralism of authority. He regards leadership as the highest form of participative management and his doors are always open to any of his managers seeking his guidance on any knotty issue. The leader must never forget his role as a visionary. Vision is not just thinking about the future but also focusing on the long term.

A leader cannot rest on laurels for his past experience. New frontiers of knowledge are opening up all the time and today's leader has to be alive to the developments in the spheres of economy, polity, education, health, public services and environment because these affect all human establishments including the business enterprise in his charge. In the age of knowledge, a leader takes a calculated risk and not a blind jump. If he is not well informed, he will end up looking foolhardy, not enterprising, while handling an untested turf. Today's leader looks ahead and takes initiative to reach out to information. If he is regarded as trustworthy, it is in the sense that he cannot be faulted for ignorance. He instinctively takes the right decision at the right time precisely because he has the advantage of being knowledgeable. Today, businesses need information-focused leadership. Managing information is perhaps the most important instrument of success in business and has to become a function of the firm's leadership. The leader must have knowledge of the different aspects of today's inter-dependent world as well as a global mindset sustained by such knowledge. A leader encourages knowledge creation and understands that one has to spend on securing new information.

Decisiveness is a fundamental attribute of an effective leadership. In the age of information, decisions are knowledge-based and since the dynamics of globalization can produce new facts and data, it can potentially alter a major plank on which the earlier decision was based. A leader today may, therefore, have to shift his stance after making a choice. He should not hesitate to change course and revise an earlier decision, to meet the new strategic compulsion. If he enjoys trustworthiness, has the image of being pro-active, commands respect for being a man of nerves, and retains a reputation for being knowledgeable, his changing a decision would not detract from the organizational energy required for the implementation of the new plan. Leadership of an intelligent enterprise is free to revise a decision provided it keeps the organization convinced that the change of course is dictated by new knowledge or developments.

The leader understands that all business is human activity and views the employees as a permanent resource. He constantly upgrades them through training and assignment to new operations and makes them an instrument of competitive advantage. He creates a context in which there is constant quest for excellence and enhancing the firm's advantage is viewed as something normal and expected. He is convinced that the competitive gain results basically from improvement, innovation and change. A leader has a total understanding of the entire value system of his business. He is a good communicator. He can listen to the workers on the shop floor and also deliver a message that is clear enough to be understood in the organization and powerful enough to motivate the members to carry out the firm's mandate.

A business leader perceives an opportunity and also reads the signs of a threat that others have not noticed. He does not miss out on an early bird advantage because he monitors the needs of the market, trends in the industry, and the configuration of environmental forces. He likewise picks up any early warning signals and is able to prepare a strategic pre-emptive response to the doings of the rival if these are the source of an impending threat.

A good business leader never embraces a victim's mentality. In these times when stability is not the norm, heading a business is no less than leading a combat with the adversaries who may or may not be visible.

A leader seeks to transform his business into a winning organization not only in the present but also for the future so that the firm will lead even when he is not around. It is for this reason that he nurtures talent and creates leadership within the enterprise. An important task of the leader is to keep up the loyalty of his followers and wards towards his organization. A 1998 FBI study on the loss of trade secrets by Fortune 500 companies in the US revealed that in nearly 36 per cent of the cases, this was caused by a conspiring insider. Loyalty to an establishment is the product of one's own commitment to a value system on one hand and the feel good factor that the enterprise concerned is able to create amongst its personnel, on the other. A lingering grievance leads to disgruntlement that in turn, destroys loyalty. Grouse, greed and external pressure can damage loyalty, and the leader should be watchful enough to ensure that the management system of his firm deals with the concerned individuals promptly. In the competitive business environment where industrial espionage is practiced in a significant measure, creating corporate loyalty is a direct responsibility of the business leader.

A successful business leader has his human resource development people design imaginative programmes to focus a great deal on loyalty enhancement. Projection of a shared vision, a transparent system of credit-sharing, and an orientation to the thought that the economic security of the individual member lies in the security of the organization, are some of the things that can help the business leader to build an ethical organization that guarantees loyalty. This loyalty is rooted in the feel good factor that would run through the entire enterprise of this kind.

Conclusion

The five essentials of leadership in business are decision-making, reliability, initiative, nerves and knowledge base. The Indian thought attaches importance to a person's spiritual maturity that determines the capacity to look at things from a higher plane in all situations thereby facilitating macro-vision. It enhances comprehension which in turn, enables the leader to read new meanings in the facts presented to him and discover new connectivities behind events and their consequences. This gives a new edge to the decision-making. In the age of knowledge, a leader has to be well-informed so that he can take a calculated risk but not a blind jump. He must encourage knowledge creation and provide a context in which there is constant quest for excellence. He understands that competitive gain is achieved basically through improvement, innovation and change. Above all, a business leader is tested for his success in perceiving an opportunity and reading the signs of a threat that others may not have noticed.

References

1. '*Intelligence– A security weapon*' by D.C. Pathak, Manas Publications, Delhi 2003.
2. *The Bhagavadgita* by S. Radhakrishnan, page 127, Blackie and Son, Bombay, 1948.
3. *Maxims of Chanakya* by V.K. Subramanian, page 112, Abhinav Publications, New Delhi, 1980.

12

Communication of Intelligence

- **Knowledge is evolutionary because it can only take you forward**

If analysis of information yields competitive intelligence or the knowledge that becomes the base for vital strategic decisions, it is clear that this intelligence should be made available to the decision-makers without avoidable loss of time. It is necessary that intelligence is conveyed to the action takers in an appropriate form. In the context of intelligence, report writing is an important exercise and it is governed by some well defined principles. The report should be concise but brevity should never be at the cost of clarity. The analytical readings that constitute the content of intelligence must unfold themselves from the facts arranged in sequential layers. The decision-makers should have the freedom to go into the background material which should always be there in the form of annexures. The readings of the analysts should emanate from the objective facts of information and there should be no tendency to 'tailor' the findings to put them in tune with what the leaders of the enterprise would like to hear.

In the business world, decisions, if not taken in time, can cause grave setbacks. Many failures of intelligence result not from lack of availability of information but from the delay that creeps into its dissemination to the right quarters. Intelligence is information for action and its utility is marred if it is not presented properly, not passed on in time, or is not acted upon wisely. A successful corporation must have a system that allows flawless communication of information from one key point to another. Without such an arrangement, the growth of the enterprise would be put in jeopardy. Information flows are the life-line of modern business. A good communication is worded in simple terms. Every recipient of a message may not be attentive enough to grasp it fully in its first communication. Effective information transfer needs repetition.

Communication is important in all areas of corporate activity. In the sphere of knowledge management, it is now clearly established that the most in-depth knowledge of the external world or the competitors may be housed in the heads of people who are not necessarily high in the organization's hierarchy. Sales people who spend time out in the field know quite a lot about what competitors are doing. Your suppliers and buyers have fairly accurate perceptions of the market place. Your floor supervisors have ideas on how your operations can be improved. They are all waiting to be drawn into inter-active moments which can be used by the firm to access the tacit knowledge carried by them. The organization has to create the right system and the right atmospherics to bring this about. The corporate world can learn a lesson or two from the classical intelligence organization which runs on an extremely well developed tradition of vertical interaction between the highest supervisors and the lowest operators. This is designed to maximise productivity.

Best products and services can face a demise if nobody has communicated effectively about them. The firm should be able to get the right message to the right people at the right time. The best promotion of a product is when it is based on the truth well told. A sure source of competitive advantage lies in establishing that what you communicate is reliable. Remember, what is excellent will be recommended at its back.

Today, a large number of Fortune companies in the West employ specific staff for monitoring competitive activities. Competitive intelligence is becoming an integral part of all major players in the global business. An average executive is however still a poor information manager. Even business schools have not really kept up with the study of the changing role of information and offer no specific education programmes on this vital area of a firm's life. Most business problems can be handled if there is adequate information to facilitate the right response. Information of intelligence value has to constantly flow to the strategic analysts and the decision-makers of the firm. Competitive intelligence is a commodity on the move and the system of communication in the firm has to be swift enough to put it to an effective use.

Presentation of intelligence is becoming increasingly important in these days of compressed time schedules. Long reports dilating on charts and survey details are on a discount because the decision-maker wants to focus on the findings, make some queries he thinks he should make to feel comfortable with the credibility of the research, and put the points of analysis to use for exercising the choice of strategic option. The merit of presentation depends on the quality of communication, designing of graphics and visuals meant to explain the finding and its roots, and the clarity with which it projects the competitive advantage that a suggested course of action would bring to the firm. Intelligence gives a firm the sense of control in leveraging its advantages. It gives the empowerment that it needs. It is therefore of crucial importance that intelligence does not remain undelivered because of any flaw of communication.

In the age of knowledge, information about the corporate gains as well as the setbacks if any, must be shared with the employees and other stake-holders. Internal communications establish transparency, promote an ethical orientation of the organizational culture, and generally sustain the morale of the work force. Unambiguous, objective, and timely communication helps in all situations – in normal times and in challenging moments. Gaps in communication are known to have caused avoidable damage by encouraging office gossip, rumours and misrepresentations about the enterprise. The internal communications, of course, have to accommodate the principles of restrictive security and protection of proprietary information.

Communication is the most important medium of governance. Leaders have to be effective communicators and subordinates have to be encouraged to talk. A firm must create a culture where people can share information—good or bad. According to Narayan Murthy, Chairman, Infosys, the motto for work-place interactions set by him for his company is 'you can disagree with me as long as you are not disagreeable.'[1]

Communication skills are a major instrument of effective supervision which is a prime feature of any intelligent organization. In the parlance of intelligence, the senior must be competent about 'briefing' and 'debriefing.' Proper briefing ensures that the task at hand is understood well down the line. Debriefing is the communication by which the feedback travels up to the leadership of the firm. Good debriefing removes any inadequacy of reporting from below on account of diffidence, anxiety or a lack of morale. In the internet age, enormous volumes of information can travel great distances in a short span of time. An information savvy executive understands the significance of communication per se. This is important because in a contingency, communication channels can be clogged by the communicators who are overtaken by information overload.

A firm has an internal world of its own but its interaction with the world outside is the essence of its business operations. The companies communicate with the public through call centres, websites and toll free telephone numbers. The aim of external communication is to establish continuity of the firm's image in the areas of operational and financial well-being. It is essential that communication systems are tested through random checks. Every time this is done, it should lead to some further refining of the system to the advantage of the firm.

Conclusion

If the success of a business today rests on intelligence-based decisions, it goes without saying that all information of intelligence value must reach the firm's leadership in quick time. Information flows infact, are the lifeline of modern business. Timely information can avert a crisis and uncommunicated intelligence can cause a serious setback. Leaders have to be effective communicators. Since communication is the most important medium of governance, it is necessary for a firm to ensure that in a contingency communication channels never get clogged. A good communication uses a simple idiom, does not leave room for ambiguity in its interpretation, and has a flawless transmission. Also, remember that a certain degree of repetition of the message makes the information-transfer effective.

Reference

1. *Hindustan Times,* August 30, 2005.

13

Enhancing Productivity

- **In the information age, the prime quality of leadership is the ability to take knowledge-based decisions.**

An 'intelligent' organization has to be an effective organization. Being effective means performing efficiently in terms of achieving the targeted productivity within the given time-frame. An efficient performance is the outcome of an integral handling of planning, execution and the task of constantly sharpening the human instrument available to the organization. Productivity runs on five planks – competent strategic thinking and planning, clear communication of decisions or directions, participative supervision, an intrinsic sense of commitment in the employees, and a systemic feedback going up to the leadership of the enterprise.

Even when organizational capability achieves competitive productivity, there is the risk of fluctuations in profitability because of external dimensions such as a downswing of demand on account of a shift in consumer's preference or a change in the taxation laws. That is why plans have to be formulated with vision and an awareness of the strategic environment. Strategic planning needs investment of time and money. It has to be information-based and evolved out of the futuristic projections made by the firm's bright intellects. Intelligence is a basic requirement for strategic planning which, in turn, determines the prospect of success in business and industry.

The best of plans can run into faulty execution if the very first step of clearly communicating them to the staff or the work force is not taken properly. Commitment of the members is built on an unflawed understanding of the plans and directions in the first place. The process of communication has to ensure that this understanding will never be below par. This process will test the system of supervision that the organization has created for itself. If the organization is strong on participative supervision, it will cast a duty on the seniors in the hierarchy to make sure that instructions are understood down the line and that the feed-back on experience gained travels upwards all the time. Participative supervision is a major tool for building a pervasive sense of commitment within the organization.

A business organization is a living organism; it is a human system. It grows if it has a thinking head, a body that carries out the day-to-day tasks and an attitude of constantly learning from experience. A business, like the profession of intelligence is all about human activity. A corporate body can become a sure gainer if it achieves an operational sync on the basis of a sensitive oversight of the human resource and an ongoing organizational learning. A business enterprise, infact, must regard learning as among its most basic capabilities. This will keep it closer to the reality of the situation and protect it from purely speculative initiatives.

In any organization, strategic planners have a difficult task to perform. They have to have their hands on the pulse of the 'present' while thinking of the scene ahead. Evaluation of what is going on combined with the lessons of the past, can propel them into the area of anticipation for the future provided the information available to them has no significant gaps. Strategic thinking and planning have undergone a sea-change since the advent of knowledge economy. Study of the competitive environment in conjunction with the assessment of knowledge assets generated within the organization, has become a powerful tool for sculpting the right business strategies. The leadership of an enterprise today has to have a new mind-set that sees the importance of change as a harbinger of opportunity and hope.

A mission statement is what basically it should be – a statement that picturises the goal but is not a substitute for the effort that would take the enterprise to the finishing line ahead of the others. The mission is an achievable target to be consciously decided upon by the leadership of the organisation in a futuristic time-frame. Mission is a subset of the company's vision. Vision is not an illusion. It is an insight into the future, made possible by a realistic appraisal of the firm's strengths, the confidence rooted in its experience, and a pro-active disposition. Above all, however, this insight rests on a deft use of knowledge or intelligence for venturing into the unseen turf. The vision and the mission mark the success of anticipation. They set the direction of progression for the firm and define the distinct strategy of execution that the organization would adopt for this purpose.

A mission statement is not a set of generalizations or a mere recall of the principles that guarantee excellence. It is a pithy assertion of the specific mile-stones sought to be reached by the firm using the means stated therein. A mission statement is a standing reminder to every individual member of the firm, of his or her role in pushing the enterprise towards its goal with an awareness of the competitive environment. If this does not happen, then there is something amiss about the formulation of the mission statement. The test of any strategy lies in its successful implementation. An organization's leadership, therefore, lays out the mission statement and takes full responsibility for its execution. An 'intelligent' organization eliminates the malady of internal bureaucratization that creates a disconnect between the mission and its implementation and between 'ideation' and the 'hands on' experience. Such an organization also makes it clear that a goal is a measure of commitment and not a symbol of regimentation and that it can be upgraded, advanced or shifted further by way of a mid-course correction necessitated by new knowledge. Business situations are created by human beings and this creates a certain flexibility around the surest of goals.

Job security is a prime source of loyalty and hence, of optimal productivity. In today's competitive world, business entities are themselves vulnerable to the pressures for merger, restructuring, downsizing, relocation of jobs, and even an overhaul of management. This naturally creates apprehensions about a sudden change, amongst the employees. If human resource development people mount the demands for change rather than for improvement, the employees may develop anxieties about their relationship with the firm. If the company's goal can be translated into intelligible tasking for each concerned individual, the efforts to unlock the true potential of all will become more meaningful. Motivational exhortations, if they are too general, are easily forgotten but if they correlate to real-time functions of the work force, they can spur thinking and application and possibly bring about a better performance all-round. The people must know where they have to go and must feel that the whole organization is with them.

Anxiety is the anti-thesis of enthusiasm. It causes energy drain and distances the employee further from the joy of successful closure of the project at hand. A firm may not be in a position to redress sources of unhappiness in the personal realm of the employee but it should definitely incorporate in its mentoring programmes a few things that universally impact on attitudes at the work place in a positive way. One is to inject what is called a spiritual content in thinking, which in simple terms, is the inclination to take a higher view of the visible scheme of things around so that one gets a correct perspective on one's own placing in it. Life is nature's bounty that is finite and the fun of being active and productive in the given span is what is entirely 'willed' to human beings. The effort is more important than the outcome because outcomes may be determined by events that are not in the individual's control. An 'intelligent' organization values and fosters the spirit of inquiry because this creates the healthy attitude of curiosity that ensures application with a sense of purpose. If the leadership of the firm sends out this message, it will minimise the fear of failure among the employees and make them more productive.

For a firm, one way of advancing is to develop gutsy goals that make you stretch. Remember, the world is too full of people who are too scared to take chances. An enterprise known for bold initiatives makes its work force more enthusiastic about the projects at hand.

In an intelligent organization, the members are ever willing to join hands for achieving better results. There is a grid of understanding that keeps them in readiness to do this. Coordination exists only among the individuals who are fully developed in themselves. Interdependence is possible among entities that are otherwise fully independent. This self-development leading to human independence, is presaged by the optimal mix of logic and sensitivities that a person is able to acquire through the experience of human interaction. Intelligence demands a logical mind and understanding of human behaviour and emotions. The people who have these, can stay connected with others inspite of disagreements. This is a dividend of what the specialists call 'emotional intelligence,' that determines the ability to maintain satisfying interpersonal relationship. A sense of humour is a manifestation of the ability to handle a challenging human situation. A philosophy of life helps to boost this ability. A developed mind rises above the experience of the immediate to take happy and unhappy encounters as part of the wider scheme of things. The sense of achievement is in doing regardless of the final outcome. Contributing their mite to the organization's productivity comes more easily to the employees who have been awakened along this line.

It is not adequately realized that a productive company performs well because trust becomes the guiding principle of its organization. Trust is rooted in truth and truth establishes the internal transparency in which the key players of the company can hold their position only by demonstrating their capabilities and not by hiding their incompetence behind the closed door offices. Transparency, of which a fair system of credit sharing becomes an essential part, enhances the morale and commitment of the workers. This in turn adds to the overall productivity of the firm. Genuinely open communications are the vehicle that brings up the truth to everybody concerned and establishes transparency.

It is logical to say that the time spent by a firm on 'thought' and 'talk,' is inversely proportional to productive work or value addition. An intelligent business creates an action-oriented mind-set. It does not spend more time than is minimally required on the post-mortem of a failure but sets up a plan of remedial action for immediate implementation. The thinking time must be all devoted to continual improvement, examination of the feedback, evaluation of the competitive determinants, and the ways and means of creating new knowledge within the firm.

A productivity enhancer not considered by most firms is the replacement of opulence and showy perks of the bosses by an egalitarian atmosphere around the leadership. The enterprise must establish a tradition of the people at the top showing a clear inclination of working in efficient spartan surroundings. Moreover, highly productive firms run their business without the typically wasteful and cumbersome bureaucracy and remain committed to flattening the hierarchical structure. They never forget that bureaucracy makes organizations less productive.

Conclusion

Productivity is determined by competent planning, clarity about decisions, supervision of execution, commitment of workers and a constant review of progress. Strategy should be based on intelligence about the market and the competitive environ. A mission statement helps the firm to define its goal and lay down the pathway to reach it for the benefit of its entire work force. In today's competitive world, the goal sets the parameters of commitment without invoking regimentation. Participative supervision fosters the tradition in which the effort is considered more important than the outcome and the employees are made more productive by eliminating the needless fear of failure from amongst them. An intelligent organization promotes loyalty which is a prime facilitator of good performance. An intelligent business uses monitoring mechanisms for creating an action-oriented mindset and not for carrying out a postmortem of failures. Among the important productivity enhancers are a conscious reduction of wasteful bureaucracy, creation of new knowledge within the firm, attention to tasking for unlocking the true potential of every member of the organization, establishment of internal transparency, and a style of management that does not create anxieties among the workers about their relationship with the enterprise.

14

Reading the Threat

- **Prompt communication of intelligence is as important as the intelligence itself.**

An intelligent firm lays great store on foreseeing a crisis and averting it in time. It understands that this is no less important than sensing an opportunity of achieving greater profitability. The threat of industrial espionage which means a loss of trade secrets, and sabotage which is defined as 'an unacceptable physical damage caused by the enemy', are serious matters that are well understood. However, a wide range of covert dangers do exist on the horizon for businesses all the time. A potential change affecting the competitive environment may damage the company's brand value or destroy the loyalty of the customers. Managing a crisis is a crucial organizational capability but diagnosing a potential threat in time is even more important. 'It is pardonable to be defeated but not to be surprised' is a precept of war attributed to Frederick the

Great but it remains relevant to the combative corporate setting that globalization has created for businesses across the national frontiers.

Intelligence is the prior knowledge of an impending threat or crisis and it comes either as information from right sources in the right time or is the product of a competent analysis of the facts accruing from observations made within and outside the organization and the information available in the open. A major threat howsoever concealed in its origins has a period of progression before it hits its target and logically, therefore, there is always a time span – big or small, during which readable signs appear on the radar of a watchful and discerning enterprise. A crisis has an incubation period before it explodes. A big communal riot, for instance, can erupt only at the end of a period of simmering tension and an alert and watchful administration should be able to use this space for a preventive intervention on its part. A successful corporation today also has to develop this ability to read a threat. A firm may itself not be the specific target of a brewing threat but a crisis in the market has to be evaluated by that firm in order to protect it from the possible consequences of the adverse development.

The ability to read a threat is incomplete without a matching competence to launch remedial action in time. In an extremely competitive existence, the businesses are threatened by the rivals digging holes in the reputation of a product. As it is, a lot of marketing and advertising effort is needed to sustain a brand. The company has to be prepared to initiate and invest in a convincing defence of the product against an incidental or deliberate attack on its claims and merit. An impending legislative or executive order may adversely impact on the firm's operations. The strategy of response to a threat or a crisis has an important place in the scheme of things of an 'intelligent' outfit. The warning signals of a threat may appear from within the organization or they may be sighted on the horizon outside. They should be picked up and studied. A problem will not go away merely because you have ignored it. Just as a potential threat to national security detected by the intelligence organisation is met with an immediate counter-action, a corporate body must also be prepared to nip the trouble in the bud through concerted action. Resort to only a half-baked or half-hearted response to a threat will only make the organization even more vulnerable for the future.

It is a risky world and the businesses have to reckon with not only the new kind of national disasters such as the 'mad-cow' disease and SARS but also a host of man-made threats operating globally such as the new terror, sabotage of information systems, and a sudden market crash. Companies must adopt a risk assessment process that is objective and comprehensively analytical. 9/11 produced two universally applicable consequences for business. One, it put on a discount the mathematical model of assessment bringing to the fore the study of case-scenarios as the only option for futuristic analysis. The other was the transformation of the concept of corporate security to an entirely new level of challenge and a new degree of necessity.

A large corporation has several fronts or divisions exposed to a given competitive environment. They would be affected by it in their own separate ways but they all must be geared to the same grid of awareness of this environment. If this is ensured, then any incipient threat noted by one part would help to alert the entire outfit and elicit quick remedial moves. Senior echelons of management, therefore, require special orientation on competitive intelligence over and above the general management training and the specialized programmes that they have in their respective professional segments such as production, marketing and human resource development. The nature of the political environment, legal regimen, technological progress, social value system, demography, hold of the media, and the study reports available on consumer's profile or market demand, are all relevant to businesses. Any of these determinants of the competitive environment can pose a challenge to the firm. The management must develop a systemic feedback to check out on the interplay of these factors in relation to the company's business interests. The effort made in this direction should not be considered unnecessary since in these days of instant connectivity, an insignificant looking matter may escalate in no time.

A large threat that exists all the time is an attack on the brand image, the quality of the product or the reputation of the company itself. Since this can cause a quick aggravation, the defence has to be prompt and effective. In the age of knowledge, a whole lot of information about the companies and their management systems is available on the internet. Companies define their products at length to establish their credibility. The adversary can take the advantage of this situation by using analytical tools to forge a negative picture out of the openly available data and facts. An intelligent company is able to look at its own self from outside with the eyes of a neutral observer. It can keep its ears to the ground as far as perceptions of the identified stake-holders towards the firm are concerned. If an issue arises, it can become a problem in quick time. The adversary can deliberately induce a debate so that it can develop into a controversy involving the rival product. The targeted company should not wake up to this late. It should evolve an early warning system. A firm must remember that history of failures is always written in bolder letters than the record of success. In an intelligence organisation a maxim well understood is that 'you live from failure to failure' because success is presumed to be the normal outcome. A company that has a high reputation for corporate social responsibility can defend its products better against an engineered attack. An intelligent firm makes use of the media in normal times to establish that it was always consistent in its approach to the customers and that it always stood for business ethics.

Any business enterprise should objectively examine the areas of its vulnerability to hostile forces. A bank is an establishment that is exposed to the threat of hackers getting into its systems. Customers in general would be adversely impacted even by unconfirmed news of such a threat having materialized. It can create the vision of the bank collapsing for financial reasons. A bank should be aware that fraudulent e-mails and spurious websites are used to get hold of confidential or personal security information from customers with the aim of committing a financial crime. It should be sensitive enough to detect all out-of-the-normal transactions.

Large enterprises are exposed to the possibilities of strike action by workers with or without instigation from third parties outside. A new entrant commanding strength somewhere else may appear in your own market. Globalization is producing an invisible empire with defused borders which makes it possible for a rival to spring upon you from any part of the world. Political leadership exercising regulatory powers may not always be in a position to do much for the local business against the global players. If the firm keeps a proper relationship with the politico-legal regimen in the country it would be in a better position to deal with the loaded rival than would be possible for it to do, otherwise. Above all, in a large number of cases where the firms have suffered a setback, it was on account of internal irregularities or the doings of hostile insiders. It is important that the enterprise does not miss out on an internal threat, for instance, a disgruntled employee leaking out confidential information or the trade secrets of the firm to outsiders.

Conclusion

Foreseeing a danger and averting it in time is as important as cashing in on an opportunity for advancement. A crisis seldom comes without throwing up some warning signals and an intelligent firm should use this space for making a preventive intervention. A large enterprise having several fronts or divisions must make them all aware of the possibility of a shift in the competitive environ and must lay down a system of management by which any incipient threat noted by one part would be used to alert the entire outfit. There is need for education on competitive intelligence and a firm should devise specialized programmes for its executives towards this end. An intelligent company learns to look at its own self with the eyes of a neutral observer because this is how it can visualize the possible threats to the reputation of its products and to its own corporate image. It is extremely important for a firm to objectively examine the areas of its vulnerability to hostile forces such as the threat of hackers getting into the systems of a banking enterprise or the possibilities of strike action by workers of a large manufacturing plant. The firm should have a strategy of response to a threat or a crisis and should know that a half-hearted action can end up making the organization more vulnerable for the future.

15

Making the Enterprise Secure

- **We are at the threshold of the Age of Intelligence in which only intelligent organizations and enterprises converting knowledge into opportunities would survive.**

In popular perception, national security is something that is remote and totally a concern of the government. A citizen tends to relate more easily to the issues of personal safety and protection against crime. The corporate world, the life-line of the country's economic progress, likewise lives in its own vision of sales and gains with a package of expectations from the government to help it out in making even greater profits. It vaguely relies on the State to provide it with complete security but is hardly interested in the strategic scenario that envelops the nation. Now that it is becoming increasingly clear that economic security is an integral part of the overall national security, corporate India would do well to understand the facets of national security in the interest of its own well-being.

In the age of information, no corporate employee will be complete as a knowledge worker without having an idea of the fundamentals of national security. The interplay of information technology revolution and the security issues itself is a matter that has to be brought within the area of awareness of every corporate entity today. We are moving towards a global economy and the buzz word is 'interdependence.' A proper give and take, however, can take place in international interactions only among fully developed entities who have a matching capacity to deliver, on the one hand, and the ability to understand the intentions of the other parties, on the other. An awareness of national security concerns is important for the corporate representatives engaging in transnational and international activity. It should not come to anybody as a surprise that businesses can unwittingly provide the 'cover' for someone's unseen activities at the behest of an adversary. The corporate enterprises, whether in public or private sector, should develop a good understanding of the new security environ that prevails in the world since the end of the cold war.

The age of information has coincided with the rise of the global terror. 9/11 was an assault on the identity of the US as a political and economic superpower. It can be said that global business enterprises are now generally vulnerable to the threat of terrorism depending on whether they are identified with a country targeted by some terrorist group or the other. There is rapid rise of another kind of risk posed to the business enterprises by organized criminal gangs practising a terrorist methodology. These trends are perhaps not being adequately studied by the business world. In December 2004, an Assistant Manager of Northern Bank in Belfast, Northern Ireland was picked up by criminals dressed up as police officers, from his residence and his wife was also kidnapped and held hostage to make the bankman help, at the point of gun, the operation of a fifty million dollar bank robbery. Threatening calls, car jacking and kidnapping for extortion are the emerging crimes directed against top executives of private and public sector undertakings. They are challenging corporate security in a manner that is entirely new. The function of the chief security officer of a firm has become extremely important for securing not only the enterprise and its operations but also its top leadership.

A country is weakened by its enemy through the clandestine means of 'espionage' or an unauthorized access to the State secrets, 'subversion' of the population which, in essence, is the destruction of the loyalty of the people towards the State, and 'sabotage' which is the word for physical damage caused to the national assets on an unacceptable scale. The proxy war being conducted by a hostile neighbour against India began with the targeting of economic assets in the serial bomb blasts in Mumbai in 1993. Corporate security, likewise, means protection against the unseen threats from outside the organization or from within, in the form of industrial espionage i.e. theft of trade secrets, subversion of the work force and sabotage by way of destruction of machinery, stores or the information system of the enterprise. For each of these threats, a specific security package has to be put in place. It is important to note that security is for prevention and not for post-event inquiry into the damage caused. The system put in use should have a correlation with the threats and should be made cost-effective.

It is now being acknowledged that corporate security is a management function drawing its empowerment from the head of the organization. Security should not be regarded as a necessary evil but as a helpful instrument for safeguarding productivity and enhancing the worker's loyalty. It is important for the organization to establish a strong management culture in which the personnel take security controls seriously. A good security system should be overseen by a top functionary of the corporate body on behalf of the chief of the enterprise.

The first step in building a security system is to establish a fail-safe perimeter or physical security which prevents a frontal threat from materializing and which is much more than employing a few guards in uniform at the main entrance of the premises where the enterprise is located. The physical security package has three essentials parts – a security fencing with an intrusion alarm backup, a system of admittance at the defined entry points through identification, and the inside 'access controls' to safeguard the vulnerable points within the establishment through a system of fresh identification.

Trade secret losses in the US alone amounted to nearly 24 billion dollars annually in the Nineties. If espionage is unauthorized access to protected information, then it is clear that an enterprise must protect its proprietary information through a system of security classification and procedures for access authorization. Not many executives realize the importance of this security requirement. They do not ensure the destruction of papers containing corrected drafts of sensitive communications and orders. There is not enough realization in the corporate world that a desktop shredder should be part of the standard office equipment of a senior manager.

Information technology is demolishing national boundaries with the result that the theft of proprietary information has emerged as a prime threat to commercial and strategic assets. Even the future wars, it is realized, will be fought away from the front line – in cyber space, as the enemy targets the information systems of the opponent. The growing IT industry of India needs to keep abreast of the newer threats of network breaches and build an effective system of security against them.

Subversion basically means destroying the loyalty of a member to his organization. It is a means by which the enemy can achieve the objective of espionage or even sabotage. It is a matter of satisfaction that corporate bodies are becoming increasingly aware of the need to keep their personnel protected from the invisible advances of the hostile rival at home and abroad. Social engineering techniques are employed by the enemy not only to ferret out information from the members of a target organization but even to win them over eventually for more sinister objectives. A 1998 FBI study found that 36 per cent of American corporations experienced unauthorized access of their systems by insiders. The importance of personnel security in enhancing the collective security consciousness is still not adequately understood. Personnel security is strengthened if background checks are made on new entrants, loyalty programmes are conducted within the enterprise, and a 'need to know' methodology defined in professional terms as 'restrictive security' is put in place.

With the advent of the new global terror in the Nineties, an aspect of corporate security hitherto considered obscure has become contextually live. Agents of terrorism could position themselves as employees of business concerns and use the 'cover' to run their operations. One of the suspects in the Diwali-eve serial bomb blasts in New Delhi on October 29, 2005 worked as the sales representative of a well known multinational concern.

Once the security concepts are grasped by the corporate leadership, it becomes easy to establish a cost-effective security infrastructure for the enterprise. Security management must become a part of the overall business management. This is all the more necessary because security management has now acquired a strategic economic significance. Security awareness binds the members of a corporate body together and strengthens their perception that their own security and well-being lie in the security and economic resilience of their enterprise. This is a powerful source of loyalty. A loyal member of the corporation, willingly adhering to the security code of which punctuality will always be an integral part, would add to the productivity. As important as the creation of a security setup is the establishment of a management culture that values security.

Since security is 'a matter of degree,' there has to be a constant upgrading of the security system on the basis of a security audit and a review of the new information being received about threats. The corporate leadership should learn to provide an appropriate budget for making the business enterprise secure. The requirements of security go beyond a mere theft by an employee or someone else, to the realm of building protection against the larger threats of espionage, subversion, and sabotage. A security system needs a reasonable one time initial capital expenditure on constructions, gadgetry and hiring of the personnel and the subsequent recurring expenditure on a much smaller scale on salaries, maintenance and upgradation.

Tighter security is needed when the firm is in the midst of a difficulty. During such a period, front reception basically needs to be strengthened and the areas vulnerable to the new challenge require to be given an extra cover. It is equally important that employees are specially briefed on how to prevent leaks of sensitive information as there would be a likelihood of rivals stepping up their effort to pry into the internal goings-on of that firm.

A ten-point guideline can be laid down for those whose responsibility it is to organize the security of the key leaders of their enterprise. First, security is not a question of attaching a muscleman in uniform to be with the protectee all the time, but is a function of intelligence designed to prevent or neutralize a surreptitious assault. Since the attack on the protectee would be a planned one, the security man has to be trained well enough to pick up any warning signals that could be there in many cases.

Secondly, as in any security exercise, a risk analysis must be made to assess the threat environment facing the enterprise and the kind of crimes and dangerous situations to which the key leader of that outfit is vulnerable. Thirdly, the security man has to have a fairly comprehensive idea of the area of movement of the protected person both in the official as well as the private time, particularly of its parts that are known to the outsiders. Sometimes a lot of information useful to the potential attacker is available on the company's website. All that has to be examined to identify the vulnerable points in the protectee's routine will require further attention.

Fourthly, security has to be unobtrusive to find acceptance. The security man himself is a physically fit person of education and intelligence orientation who has skills like defensive driving and ability to direct counter-surveillance moves. He blends into the executive's milieu and does not allow security to become an impediment to the latter's activity and movement. Fifthly, the people handling security also have the added responsibility of developing among the protectees the right degree of awareness and sensitivity towards the issues of protection against dangers that are well understood.

Sixthly, good security makes good use of technology. Technology is a force multiplier. It enhances the remote control, facilitates speedy responses, and acts as an economizer for the operations in the long term. Seventhly, since there is always a scope for improving security in keeping with the developing threat scenario, study of the new threats should be kept up and lessons taken even from the experiences of others in the field.

Eighthly, the immediate family of the protectee are also a good target for the terrorist and criminal gangs. Security of the leader therefore, would not be complete without adequate cover being provided to his spouse and children. Ninthly, security must be cost-effective and must not degenerate into an index of glamour or become an instrument of display of status. Since the value of investment on security cannot be assessed in terms of intelligible results, an enterprise would be reluctant to allocate separate funds for it. However, in the present global security scenario, firms have to learn to set apart such funds as part of the planned expenditure.

Lastly, the enterprise must adopt a culture of security and the members, high and low, must willingly abide by the prescribed do's and don'ts so that the security of the firm and the protection of its leaders complement each other. Security orientation should, therefore, become a part of the human resource development. While security infrastructure has to use specially trained manpower, a good strategy should encourage voluntary sharing of security duties by the general employees as well. Moreover, it might be a good idea to recruit security personnel from amongst the wards of the old employees as this brings in loyalty and also adds to the nurtural image of the enterprise.

In the age of globalization, the dividing line between national security and economic security of the country is thinning out. Corporate security should, therefore, be in tune with the initiatives that the government takes in the area of maintaining the wider security of the nation. A natural grid of cooperation and understanding should exist between them. In the race towards the new economic order we have to keep up the stability of the individual, the institution, and the corporate entity. National security is now a holistic concept and requires integral responses across the spheres of politics, economy, and defence. Corporate management today has to understand the nuances of national and global security for its own advantage.

Conclusion

No corporate employee today can be regarded as a knowledge worker if he or she does not have an idea of the fundamentals of national security and an understanding of the national security concerns of our times. Apart from terrorism, the rise of criminal mafia indulging in kidnapping for ransom, and the advent of cyber crimes, have added new dimensions to corporate security. The threats of espionage, subversion and sabotage face the public and private sector alike. A firm needs to make a reasonable one-time capital expenditure on installing a cost-effective security system which can then be run on a much smaller recurring expenditure. Industrial security means much more than employing a few guards in uniform at the main entrance of the premises. In a large proportion of cases, security is damaged by a colluding insider. The firm, therefore, needs a combination of physical, personnel and information-security measures commensurate with the risk analysis made for it. Corporate security has to be a top management function as it covers all aspects of the firm – organizational and operational. It needs a periodical review since the security scenario can change because of the advent of new threats.

16

Business Vigilance

- **In the information age no corporate employee will be complete as a knowledge worker without having an idea of the fundamentals of security.**

Just as corporate security is meant to operate against the invisible threat engineered by the adversary or an enemy outside, vigilance is against the possibilities of damage to be caused by the organization's own members. Insiders are known to have seriously hurt their own enterprise after they have fallen to greed, have become disgruntled, or come under the influence of a rival. Such elements willfully violate the norms and procedures set by the firm for an ulterior motive and cause grave financial losses to it. Vigilance is becoming an integral part of corporate governance, particularly in the wake of an unusual number of internal scams and frauds witnessed by some leading global corporations. Time has come for every business school to step up the discourse on regulations, ethics, integrity, transparency, and personal values.

Ranging from Enron to WorldCom to Tyco and so many others, global giants have had their corporate image destroyed by blatant corruption. Their top people have been charged with accounting frauds that went undetected for years. They burnished and distorted financial results of their companies for building their personal fortunes. The former Chairman of collapsed South Korean conglomerate, the Daewoo Group was indicted in July 2005 on fraud charges worth US 71 billion dollars. He had fled South Korea in 1999. He was accused of having falsified Daewoo's accounts to draw billions of dollars in illegal bank loans before diverting them overseas.[1] A view is emerging that a misdemeanour of scale cannot be committed in a firm without the implicit knowledge of its top leadership. Security and Exchange Commissions and their counterparts are therefore beginning to devise methods of increasing the accountability of the Board of Directors of a business organization in the area of scrutinizing the firm's financial statements.

The corporate world is waking up to the need for internal vigilance and internal transparency in the conduct of business. The concept of vigilance has hitherto been in vogue in the government departments or public sector enterprises because corruption essentially is the misuse of the authority of the State for diverting profits to one's own pockets. The vigilance setup in such an outfit has the external backing of the State —the ultimate 'owner.' In a private corporate setting, a need is now felt for an internal vigilance machinery of the enterprise set up on the direct authority of the top man. Except for the unusual situation where the chief of the enterprise himself is involved in irregularities, the internal vigilance machinery of the firm will be able to play an effective role in ensuring that the do's and don't's laid down by the leadership are followed, provided that it derives authority from the top and is responsible to the person at the apex. In a transparent and ethical internal management of the firm, lies the best guarantee of personal rectitude of all its members. It would be a natural corollary of the vigilance function to try to enhance the awareness of the entire organization towards the ethical code of conduct prescribed for its functionaries.

A value system for corporate management fits in with the concept that a corporation needs to be recognized as a 'corporate citizen.' Implicit in this is the principle that a corporate body must also live up to its obligations towards the State and that its operations should not be in contradiction with the interests of the nation. In times to come, individuals, organizations, and nations will all need the stability that only an ethical conduct all round is able to establish. In the era of globalization, competition need not rest on the negative thought that ends justify the means. Ethical corporations would on the other hand understand each other better and will be more attuned to working in sync for the larger good of them all. Honest joint ventures will help to complement all the partners. The cut-throat combativeness will yield to friendly co-branding and alliances. A business corporation cannot evade its responsibility towards the society in which it operates. The issues of environment, social welfare, and contribution to the national economy are now in full view and they will demand clear affirmations in the corporation's charter and vision.

An ethical corporation runs good chances of producing in-house leaders who come to the top on the strength of learning and experience. They enjoy acceptance because they move up the ladder with a demonstrable merit. They can deliver because they have the knowledge of how to get the best out of the staff. They pitch on a vision that they know they can achieve for the organization they lead. They are not the 'celebrity rainmakers' or short term super executives brought in by many firms from outside to shake things up and send that stock in the right direction. Competitiveness has given rise to a culture of corporate star-gazing characterized by unrealistic expectations and swift punishment for failure. That is why there has been a fast turn-over of CEOs in major firms in recent years. An ethical corporation helps to create stability at the top because everybody down the line is reasonably free of misgivings about decision-making and willing to push ahead with a sense of confidence and loyalty. A firm is a human unit whose thinking head and the working limbs are in consonance with each other. Business vigilance keeps a check on willful violations that obstruct the smooth running of the corporation by disturbing this rhythm.

In a government organization or a public sector enterprise, the head of the vigilance setup even while holding a senior position does not sometimes get to enjoy the confidence of the top man – the chairman-cum-managing director of the corporation, merely because the latter is distrustful of the chief vigilance officer's direct access to the authority outside the enterprise. Unless the vigilance setup makes it a point not to send any communication to an authority outside the firm, without prior knowledge of the top man, this impediment will remain and the vigilance chief will not get the kind of support he needs from the head of the undertaking. Unless there are some definite reasons for the CVO to do otherwise, he must route all his reporting through the CMD. In the private sector, the vigilance function will directly be under the top man and will deliver results. In a public-sector setting also, the CMD would like to do what is best for the organization and the vigilance setup there should be on his side. It need not take on the top man on the latter's exercise of discretion in such matters as the handling of a minor or unintended deviation from the laid down norms of procedure. The CMD's judgment on what impacts on the overall performance of the enterprise should be respected. In a government controlled sector, the vigilance setup is sometimes keen to buy its importance by flaunting its power to get an inquiry launched even into a small procedural flaw. It should not function in a manner that dampens the initiative of the employees to attempt an innovation or exercise an independent decision-making. Nothing should be done that detracts from the competitiveness of a company in the government's control in relation to its counterpart in the private sector.

It is interesting that it is in the age of globalization with its new levels of competitiveness, that the need for corporate governance resting on the foundations of business ethics, has been felt most acutely. The blatant corruption of the kings of the business world like Kenneth Lay, Jeffrey Skilling and Bernard Ebbers, not to forget Ketan Parekh and Harshad Mehta of India, has woken up the stake-holders everywhere to the new low of unethical conduct that the powerful among the global players in business could sink to. This has impacted on the people's faith in the guardianship of the government in the area of protecting the hard earned money of the common man. There is a rapid move towards a universal consensus that corporate ethics alone can provide the level playing field so necessary for the advance of globalized economy. In India, companies like Infosys and Wipro have taken new initiatives in this direction. Wipro, for instance, is said to have adopted a detailed Integrity Manual which, among other things, discourages advertisements that unfairly disparage the products or services of competitors. An ethical corporation can hope to gain internally as also in its dealings with outsiders. The business world will have to realize that exercising ethical options is not about sainthood but about sanity.

The movement for upgrading the accountability of the board of governors in the corporate bodies is a welcome development. The chief executive officer's arbitrary powers need to be placed under greater scrutiny of a collectivity of minds at the top. At the board level itself, the notions of perks without work are undergoing a change as the board is gradually becoming a symbol of participative supervision right at the company's apex. Integrity and transparency flow from the top. It is in the fitness of things that in both USA and India, Stock Exchange bodies are stepping up their efforts to monitor the working of corporations to check any mal-practices on their part in such areas as stock valuation, recording of profits, and placement of accounts before the annual general body meetings. It will be a good idea if the corporate bodies make public declaration of the total compensations that they pay to their top-bracket functionaries.

Every business school today must also talk about laws, regulations, ethics, integrity and personal values. Money and power can both have a corrupting influence. There will be temptations to misuse knowledge and authority which can be resisted only on the strength of character. Remember that even if the world fails to notice your fall for greed, your inner personality will be damaged by it. Excellence cannot be achieved by people who have serious flaws of character.

A vigilance setup in a corporation will really serve no purpose if it only allows the subordinates to be punished routinely without even going into a thorough examination and questioning of the role of the seniors exercising the oversight function in relation to the indicted employees. In the departments of the government and the public sector undertakings in India, legal protection is available to the top bureaucrats in vigilance cases by way of a provision that makes the prior permission of the government an essential requisite for taking up any case against them. The consequences of this extra insulation from charges of malpractice and corruption, in terms of costs to the government, have to be carefully calculated. For business corporations in the private sector, lack of accountability for comprehensive supervision can certainly prove disastrous. If there is a serious system failure at one level, the supervising personnel immediately above cannot escape some implicit blame. An honest internal analysis of the event must in any case be made to set in motion a corrective response and strategy for the future. The inherent competence and standing of a vigilance setup lies in its ability to certify the innocence of a member after a quick inquiry fails to establish any case of misdemeanour. The opposite of this happens most of the time and the vigilance people end up pursuing minor violations of procedure to needless length. They become infamous for their nuisance value in the process.

The senior manager must spend some time in the work area or on the operational canvas. Only participative supervision can help to pre-empt bottlenecks. Post-event inquiries cannot neutralize the damage already done. Availability of hands-on guidance at all levels of management is a must for a modern progressive company. It takes away fear of failure and releases the dormant energy of the employees for showing initiative and trying out an innovative approach. In a classical intelligence organization, the top man is accessible for consultation and advice all the time but there is complete operational freedom down the line. If the supervision is not inquisitory and is supportive and nurtural, it serves the cause of business vigilance itself.

An important aim of any enterprise today is to encourage individual performers who can make value addition to the business operations by creating new learning. Strategies for human resource development have acquired a new meaning. Corporate loyalty is an interesting but complex area of study in this context. The importance of investment on staff for their improvement both financially and in terms of their emotional well-being has increased. By eliminating the bad fish, the vigilance setup helps to create an environment in which the level of commitment to the firm outweighs, to an extent, the desire of the member to cross over to another organization merely for a little more salary. Loyalty is a matter of identification with the organization and it develops principally when there is internal transparency in the firm about credit sharing and reprimand. This happens when there is primacy of the ethical code. Business vigilance promotes these important determinants of corporate governance. Internal vigilance in an appropriate form must exist in all firms. We need ethical corporations who compete without taking recourse to fraudulent practices and who succeed on the strength of a genuine admiration of their stake-holders. So, establish legal and ethical ground rules for your company. Remember, the price for playing a game with different rules can be very high.

Conclusion

A rising threat to corporate security is the damage caused by the organization's own members to the economic health of the enterprise by way of corrupt practices. Corruption is the misuse of authorized office for diverting profits to one's own pockets out of greed. The concept of vigilance to counter this threat was so far in vogue more in the government departments or public sector undertakings, partly because the loss suffered by the State was too invisible or abstract to be detected immediately. The corporate world is waking up to the need for internal vigilance as many global giants – ranging from Enron to World Com, have lately had their corporate image destroyed by blatant corruption in which their top people distorted financial results of their companies for building their personal fortunes. The vigilance setup must derive its authority from the top, must have the power to carry out random scrutiny of any deal or agreement being entered into by the enterprise, and must run in-house programmes for enhancing the awareness of the ethical code of conduct prescribed by the company for its functionaries. However, nothing should be done in the name of vigilance to dampen the initiative of the employees to try out an innovation or exercise an independent judgment. A welcome development in the area of vigilance is the movement for upgrading the accountability of the board of governors in the corporate bodies.

Reference

1. *Hindustan Times*, Delhi, July 2005.

17

Information Security

- **Knowledge creation needs investment.**

In a world that is ruled by information today, knowledge of ideas, processes and technology enables one player in business to outsmart another. Corporate governance in these times requires consolidation of knowledge as an organizational resource, an on-going effort to secure such information from outside as is necessary for the firm's strategic decisions, and a clear understanding among all the members, of the business ethics of the organization they serve. It has become vital for any enterprise to safeguard its knowledge assets comprising its trade-secrets and proprietary information. Over and above the protection secured under the Patent Laws, three major areas of vulnerability have to be given attention in the context of the security of information. One is the safe storage of information, the other is the check against any intrusion on the information route and the third is the adoption of a sound 'exit policy' so that there is adequate deterrence on an employee who could, on leaving the firm, think of passing on vital business information of that enterprise to a rival company.

Security, whether it is national security or cyber security, is a matter of protection against certain kinds of clandestine threats. These include unauthorized access to the business secrets of a firm, winning over of an employee to serve some ulterior purpose of a hostile outsider, and critical damage inflicted on the information system of the enterprise by its enemy. According to a 1997 survey of US companies by the American Society for Industrial Security, losses attributed to information theft amounted to more than 250 billion dollars that year. The threat of somebody making an unathorized access to a business organization's protected information is called industrial espionage. An idea of the extent of subversion of the employees that goes on in the business firms can be had from the fact that in the US more than one third of the firms experienced breach of their systems by insiders. Physical damage on a critical scale or sabotage as it is called, can be in the form of a range of assaults from data destruction to hurting customer relations by using such techniques as false ordering, 'denial of service,' and use of e-mail bombs.

It may be mentioned that the US government continues to retain overall control of the technology which powers the internet – its domain name system, root servers and the oversight of the California-based not-for-profit Internet Corporation for Assigned Names and Numbers (ICANN) which looks after it all. There are issues of inter-governmental responsibilities for the manner the Internet is run but, in view of the rising threats of global terror and the IT-enabled organized crime, the global oversight on the internet is not to be weakened.[2]

Cyber security rests on a combination of technological and human paradigms. Information security is adversely affected by three basic shortcomings – lack of a clear security policy, gap between security policy and security practice, and inadequacy of security administration. A 1998 FBI report described mismanagement as the foremost reason for security breaches. A common dilemma is that 'policy' is often pitched at high cost and minimal risk but 'practice' operates at medium cost and risk. Two other generic determinants of the efficacy of the cyber security framework are the laxity at the physical layer which is the layer that performs physical transfer of bits to the transmission medium, and the lack of awareness of the importance of 'restrictive security' or the 'need to know' principle which is crucial in any system. Willingness to share information within the organization is looked upon as an index of internal harmony and transparency but it does not have to overturn the call of security that warrants certain sensitive information to be kept restricted beyond the reach of those who alone need to have it. A general weakness creeps into the cyber security even in strongly guarded systems because of the negligence that is commonly seen in such matters as keeping floppy disks and hard drive backup material in safe custody and destroying by shredding printed unclaimed and sensitive draft documents wherever necessary.

Measures for information security fall into three categories – physical, electronic or virtual, and personnel. The physical measures revolve round the triple combination of physical barriers, regulation of entry, and proper disposal of trash which is basically a protection against 'dumpster divers.' The electronic measures also have a threefold requirement of Access controls, Authentication and Encryption. Personnel security depends on good selection, close supervision and a meaningful security awareness training. Good security means preventing a breach and detecting in time any misuse of the system through an efficient monitoring of the system behaviour. Contingency planning and incident handling procedures should be in place and they should immediately come into play in the event of a breach.

Physical security begins with a secure site design which ensures that there would be suitable lighting, power supply, water damage protection, fire detection and suppression systems and proper ducting holes of A.C. system to prevent intrusion of any kind. External walls should be of reinforced concrete to resist forcible attack and prescribed physical barriers should be in place – from locked gates to filing cabinets. A system of regulation of entry has to be formulated through use of guards and appropriate identification. Photo I-cards are rightly being replaced by smart cards carrying biometric features of the employee. A combination of index fingerprints and face profile is coming into practice and in more sensitive situations, even iris recognition is being brought into use. Entry to sensitive sections within the premises of the enterprise has to be regulated through a second identification and authorization.

In the virtual world, the most important requirement of security is to identify proprietary information and decide which individuals would have access to it. Intellectual property is the information that gives an organization advantage over the competitors. The security policy should determine the security classification system by which the grade of security like 'secret,' 'confidential,' 'for internal circulation only' would be applied to a piece of information or to a document, and define access controls including computer and network log-in controls, firewalls, and application layer controls that would be brought into use. These are refined generic controls which become more effective when the concept of 'restrictive security' or 'need to know' is put in place. Access controls, have no meaning without authentication mechanisms that validate the identity of users. This validation is necessary so that cyber thieves are not able to impersonate legitimate users. Authentication is achieved through passwords, biometric devices, and digital signatures. Today, credit card fraud is pegged at a US 160 million dollars annual problem for just the top 25 on-line retailers. The terrorists who perpetrated 9 / 11 reportedly had numerous false identities and a very large number of credit cards.

If authentication for accessing protected information is of prime importance, equally crucial is the protection of information and data during transmission. Encryption is the best device for ensuring message confidentiality and checking unauthorized access during transmission. Passwords should always be sent encrypted. This is a protection against 'sniffers' – a kind of cyber bug used for eavesdropping. The level of secrecy of the encryption depends on the strength of the algorithm and the key length.

Identity and access management remains the key issue in information security. It would be wise for a firm to clearly identify key areas where the documents and communication that are most sensitive are located and to use appropriate technology to secure fresh identification and authorization of a person accessing them. There has to be an acceptable mean between risk management and seamless access. Overdoing one at the cost of the other will negatively impact on the business in the long run.

Spyware, which is the name for any software that selects private information on a computer, without authorization and sends it on to a third party, is now a widespread threat to business security. It is used for theft of passwords and other confidential information and for injecting 'worms,' 'viruses' and 'Trojan horses' to degrade a system. The companies should be aware of such risks and prevent downloading of freeware programmes by keeping their desktop computers locked and cleaning up their system with the help of anti-spyware tools.

In the matter of using security software, remember that you get what you pay for. Vendors must realize that technical soundness of security gadgets can be annulled by any setback caused to the consumer's confidence in the reliability of their performance. Equally important is the fact that this loss of confidence may result from a flaw in the security architecture of the enterprise itself or in the procedures formulated for operating the system. That is why a culture of security becomes so important for the firm. Steps required for information security have to be built into the enterprise at the time of its launch itself. Security is too important to be an after-thought.

Security is primarily for prevention of a breach, not for its detection though the latter is also important. No amount of post-event inquiry into a failure can make up for the loss already incurred. In electronic security therefore, intrusion and misuse detection systems become extremely important. They largely bank on a monitoring of the system behaviour. A firm should be strong in contingency-planning and incident-handling so that it can respond well to a suspected breach.

A major proportion of the crimes resulting in losses of trade secrets are committed by 'insiders.' Temptation to commit fraud for personal gain, damage done by a disgruntled employee out of spite that he harbours against the organization, and a planned attempt by the adversary to subject an employee to some kind of pressure or blackmail from outside, can be behind an inside attack. In a reported case of 1994, an employee of Ellery Systems in Colorado, USA used the internet to transfer software worth one million dollars to a competing Chinese firm. He had been given asylum in the US after the Tienamann Square incident. He was apparently influenced during a visit to China that he made subsequently. He resigned on return from that visit and then immediately effected the transfer of the data. It is possible, on the other hand, that an insider has been drawn into unconsciously revealing vital facts about his enterprise to an outsider or intruder in a situation of friendly social interaction. Social engineering techniques are used by outsiders to befriend a member invoking caste, regional or other personal commonalties. Of the same class is the use of business interaction for gaining valuable information. Clients may initiate dummy pitches to get free advice and perspectives from Consultancy and Ad services without any commitment. They pick the brains of these agencies which adds tremendous value to the client's strategic thinking and ideation process.

Three major remedial measures for ensuring personnel security in an organization are the pre-employment security vetting of employees, a suitable 'exit' policy, and the establishment of a security savvy culture within the corporate body. Security of information is best preserved when the firm establishes a management culture that understands security. The five basic concepts that buttress this understanding need to be explained. First of all, the employees at all levels must be conscious of the risks of giving away too much information. Secondly, the firm should be aware of the quantity and type of information that its business divulges in media releases, speeches, websites and other channels of communication. It should see that the classified advertisement for employment opportunities in the firm should not give away company information unnecessarily. Further, the firm must educate its trade show personnel on what information is not for public consumption. Sometimes a two day trade show yields as much competitive intelligence as a year-long intelligence gathering effort of a rival would have produced for him.

Thirdly, while using hotels or conference facility for strategic meetings, it is worth securing these premises. At conferences and seminars and even on sales calls to clients, confidential information or strategic plans of the firm should not be revealed. Enthusiastic employees can brag about the company's new product and give out information that the rival is seeking. Fourthly, if there are people in your organization who are unhappy with their current work situation, they are a potential danger to the security of the firm's protected information. The management should think of organizing counseling or some other assistance programmes for such employees. Lastly, it may not be prudent for the companies to resort too much to the threat of legal action to protect their vital interests and market position. In a legal battle, the company may have to reveal much more than what would be good for its security.

Three things are basic to a sound information security system. The security policy and security administration must have the authority of the head of the organization at their back. This will enable the system to establish a tradition of random checks and periodical audit of security. Secondly the organisation should have a strong management culture in which training and on-going briefings ensure that employees take security controls seriously. Finally, it should be realized that security is primarily preventive though it should also be detective in the sense that a breach should be instantly noticed and corrective in the sense that it should be able to indicate ways and means of fending up defences for the future in the light of the experience gained.

Most businesses today bank heavily on information technology. They need to have an administrative infrastructure to handle cyber security. An IT-based enterprise should have a steering group on internet security headed directly or indirectly by the MD himself to oversee the security administration. It has to perform three extremely important functions. It has to lay down the security policy which means identifying protected information and defining access to it. It has to establish a suitably structured security administration and approve the electronic security tools needed by the firm. Finally, it has to monitor implementation of the security policy by examining the periodical security audit reports. The security administration can be headed by GM (Operations) or some other top functionary assisted by one or two joint administrators wherever necessary. The administrator can head his own security committee to broad-base his work. The administrator is to perform three major functions. He is the custodian of security policy files, sensitive hard disks and digital signatures. He is responsible for implementation of security measures for physical, electronic and personnel security. Finally, he has to prepare security audit reports periodically through scanning of the systems for vulnerability and penetration testing. The security committee headed by security administrator should draft procedures, make relocations of responsibility at the cutting edge and organize orientation programmes on security for the staff.

With the advent of Internet in the mid-1990s computers have moved to the centre stage in companies bringing in their concerns of data security to a new centre of focus. The

CSI (Computer Security Institute) – FBI survey 2005 says that despite anti-dotes of anti-virus software and other protection mechanisms, the corporates continue to witness virus attacks as the source of greatest financial loss. It has pointed out that while security concerns are gaining priority, the security budgets of the corporates have increased only marginally. The extent of the problem can be judged from the reports that frustrated computer security firms are offering to buy tips from the very hackers who bedevil them. This is being done on the market logic that if the information comes from somebody who would have otherwise sold it on the black market, paying him something was quite in order.[1] The companies would do well to come together to fund and support an ongoing research into possible flaws in the cyber security systems being used by them so that timely action is taken to prevent the malcontents from exploiting the vulnerability. To work out global arrangements for an early warning system based on the sharing of information on malicious hackers and cyber criminals, a grand alliance was reportedly coming up between IBM, Intel, AT & T and Microsoft with FBI and the US Government. In the final analysis, a conscious and continual application of measures which strengthen information security will safeguard the firms from the invisible attacks on their systems.

Conclusion

Theft of trade secrets, clandestine attempt to damage information systems, and unauthorized access to protected information through a subverted employee, are the principal threats to information security. A combination of technological and human endeavours is needed to ensure cyber security. A firm must have a security policy and a security administration to implement it. Laxity is commonly seen in such matters as keeping floppy disks in safe custody, destroying by shredding any drafts of sensitive documents no longer in use, and consciously submitting to the practice of 'restrictive security' or 'need to know' principle which is of vital importance in any system. A prime function of security administration is to establish a management culture that understands security. In the context of cyber security the electronic measures include access controls to define which individuals in the firm would have access to the proprietary information protected by the firm through a security classification, authentication which means the procedure for validating the identity of a user, and encryption which is a way of protecting information and data during transmission. Security is primarily for prevention of a breach but the firm should also have contingency planning and incident handling procedures in place, to handle a breach.

References

1. *The Economic Times*, New Delhi, August 25, 2005.
2. *Hindustan Times*, Delhi, November 17, 2005.

18

Working Smarter

- **If two firms are performing excellently in the present, the only way one can gain over the other is by exploring the untested turf of the future.**

Nature has gifted human beings with a mind that works on the logical progression of thought. Since a business enterprise is, in essence, a collectivity of men and women, it has this immense backing of the organization's denominational strength of logic. In a situation of competitiveness, the advantage goes to the player whose sense of logic turns out to be superior. One should never presume that the rival would do anything illogical. Even the concepts of 'misinformation' and 'disinformation' used in the profession of intelligence are rooted in an analysis of what would make a logical impact on the adversary. Intelligible communications on which the inner efficiency and health of a corporate body are based, are nothing more than a logical transmission of ideas. Such communications are easy to understand because they are always in a simple idiom. 'Simplicity is the ultimate sophistication.'[1] An intelligent organization succeeds because it establishes an internal grid of logical understanding among all its members through a system of communications in which nothing can be misinterpreted or misunderstood.

In a world where the pace of change is accelerating, decision-making has become an increasingly complicated affair. Logically there is only one correct decision in any situation and in reality, it arises from the relatively few facts submerged in a mass of information, that would constitute its base. If the objective of the firm is defined with clarity, a decision about what can be done can be made more accurately. It is not generally realized that whatever is happening around us is amenable to simpler explanation than what most 'specialists' would tend to imagine. This is partly because specialization basically means more knowledge about the same and while domain knowledge, therefore, helps to make the same point in stronger terms, it does not necessarily add to the ability to see things in a broad spectrum. A business leader may have to rise above the 'specialists' to formulate an integral response to a challenge. In today's world, a sound strategy has to integrate a multiplicity of determinants that set the competitive environment.

Today, business decisions are taken against an overflow of facts and data and to pick on the right inputs for making the right decision, one requires an incisive mind that traces a logical course and an ability to filter out from the core of information, all that belongs to the fringe. Distinguishing essentials from the non-essentials and putting aside the needlessly complicated from the understandably straightforward, is a measure of rare competence. When Vilfredo Pareto, the

Italian sociologist enunciated that 'there are a significant few among the insignificant many,'[2] he was simply highlighting a principle that enables a decision-maker to work smarter. If we see without observing, observe without absorbing, and absorb without discriminating between the important and the unimportant, we go nowhere. Smartness is an ability to absorb new facts in real time and get an insight into what they mean.

For a firm, working smarter means having a better system of analyzing business information. Presuming that necessary data and facts on the competitors and the competitive environ have become available to the enterprise, these would then require to be analyzed in a competent manner to produce definitive readings or 'indicators' that can be used by the firm to take its own futuristic decisions. In short, analysis turns information into intelligence. Lack of data itself is a serious problem particularly in areas like determining the institutional and political roots of government decisions in a country or studying the factors that determine the organizational culture of the competing firms. Today a large variety of softwares are available for helping the process of sifting relevant information from a huge mass that can be tapped from the on-line data bases. A good analyst must know where to stop accumulating facts and get on to the job of collation and interpretation. The difficulties associated with intelligence analysis are often erroneously attributed to the inadequacy of available information. Firms are willing to invest on collector systems but not on enhancing analytical resources.

A smart firm, however, values competent analysis. Good business analysis rests on facts and not on wishful thinking, ideological proclivities or personal prejudices. A good analyst should be open minded about accepting new inputs which are reliable but which do not happen to fall in the familiar patterns. Western strategic analysts could not understand the strength of Shiite radicalism that had brought about the Iranian revolution of 1979 because it was a first time event. They had no experience to go by and pronounced, largely on the basis of presumption, that Ayatollah Khomeini who had established a fundamentalist regime in Tehran, would last just a few months. The Iranian cleric ruled that country as long as he lived. The pitfalls to be avoided by an analyst are a compromise with the facts under the pressures from above, inadequate examination on the plea of shortage of time, a tendency to generalize and drown the specifics in a safe statement of broad trends, injection of personal bias in the conclusions, and tailoring the findings to please the masters. In the age of information, business operations are conducted at a brisk pace and 'real time' intelligence can provide new facts about the variables in the competitive conditions. These can even cause an alteration of the strategic plan of the firm, mid-course. A smart firm understands that information updates have the potential of shortening the life span of a strategic plan.

Globalization has produced a corporate warfare. It has brought into play corporate Darwinism in which there will be survival of the fittest – not necessarily a victory for the strongest. Businesses with more funds and work force may be vanquished by smaller players who acquire a competitive edge through a smarter execution of their strategic plans. Competitive intelligence is the weapon they use to deal with their bigger looking rivals. Competition is in the minds not in the muscles. In the age of knowledge, a good strategy is always based on information of intelligence value. Often this can be churned out of the openly available facts through a competent analysis. As in any competition, the interplay of strengths and weaknesses of the two sides decides the outcome. Being smart in business also means being prompt in taking steps to quickly cut the losses arising from your weaknesses.

An intelligent business enterprise steers clear of any false sense of prestige and sheds egotism when it comes to yielding to the demand of a course correction. A smart firm knows that in a competitive business you can win not necessarily by waging a war but by bargaining and seeking mutual accommodation.[3] Here again, strategy is based on the assumption of a rational behaviour by the participants in a conflict or contest. Even nations prefer deterrence to going to war. A firm is being smart when it enters into negotiations to seek relative advantage. Its moves, however, should always be backed by good intelligence.

Businesses have over the decades been driven by the ever increasing demand of time-bound deliveries. Bosses and floor employees are both under pressure and facing their own anxieties at work. They also bring with them the stresses caused by sociological factors. An intelligent corporate body is alive to the diverse elements of the environ that impact on its workers within and outside the organization. It is prepared to share the onus of keeping its employees and managers from carrying the spill-over of the mental burdens of their personal domain to the work place. To be productive, a person needs to draw a certain degree of sustenance also in emotional and spiritual planes. A smart business enterprise provides for training on self-improvement as part of its human resource development effort. Completing the mission in hand with a devotion that is reserved for the divine, eliminating fear of failure with a conviction that having done your best you can reckon with the outcome whatever it may be, and developing credibility as a strong point of your persona, is a simple but powerful package that an intelligent organization adopts for measuring self-improvement.

It is said big ideas almost always come in small words. A little comment of an observant employee on the procedures of the enterprise, an adhoc analysis of some impediment at the assembly line by someone who is involved hands-on with it and a casual reporting on a consumer's remark on the firm's product, can contain seeds of an innovation or indicators for an epoch-making improvement. Knowledge creation is best done when the organization is able to give a fillip to new thinking and allow a certain freedom of imagination to its members to explore the larger umbrella under which the enterprise exists. The age of knowledge has transformed the concept of work force from a mass of unskilled and semi-skilled staff to a meaningful assembly of individual performers who can make value additions to the business operations by creating new learning.

A smart company develops a tradition in which the senior managers acknowledge the value of any extra effort made by the staff to strengthen the process of feedback coming to them about the experience and ideas of the workers in the shops. An intelligent enterprise has managers who discover what is unique about each person and then capitalize on it. They convert a person's particular talent into performance. In his or her area of strength, an employee will produce more in less time, making an obvious value addition thereby. A classical intelligence organization attaches a lot of importance to this reality. A run of the mill manager, however, will shun making changes and will unwittingly keep the firm from a gainful advance. Studies have shown that typical corporate executives spend only a miniscule part of their time actively thinking about the future and remain much too preoccupied with the short-term delivery to focus on the long term. The chiefs of smart firms try to solve the short-term issues within the larger perspective. They get their people on board for directing the effort to push towards the company's long-term objective. There is need for communicating with the employees on where the firm is headed. A smart firm makes this a non-stop process. BP is a good example of a global firm that brought about a turn around in the Nineties, by practising knowledge-sharing and developing organizational structures designed to ensure a free flow of information through the company. It encouraged communication among business units on the way they were grappling with similar looking problems and used IT for this. It successfully experimented with job rotation programmes which encouraged employees to move from one business unit to another so that there was internal dissemination of knowledge.

An assured system of feedback on the knowledge that exists and develops in the minds of the individual members of the firm is extremely important. The ability of the knowledge handlers of the enterprise to carryout prompt analysis of the internal information to cull out competitive intelligence from it will push the firm ahead of others. A new variant of some product feature or a process, detection of a new need or preference of the customers or an improvement in the inventory control are wanting to be discovered and the firm should be imbued with the spirit and belief that this indeed would happen. The firm's leadership must understand the pace of evolution of the intellectual property in the information economy.

An intelligent business is prepared to face the challenge of dealing with the growing multiplicity of products in the same area of consumption. It builds a consistent association of its brand with some well-defined needs of the consumer. Marlboro's attempts to extend its brand to cover several new varieties of cigarettes such as Lights, Medium and Menthol caused it some decline of market share and it had to go back to its 'real cowboy's preference' to improve matters. A smart company never gives up its known strength on a product for an uncertain line extension.

An intelligent enterprise is aware that in global markets, functional excellence cannot be achieved without an orientation towards the customer's socio-cultural responses depending on the country or region of its location. All people operate from the conditioning that their values and biases give them and not necessarily from rationality. The customer's view of the product and the message that promotes it, should be analyzed in the light of this construct. A smart firm gives its country managers a long tenure at their place and also a lot of delegated power of decision-making on behalf of the corporation. It balances this by keeping the firm structurally resilient and for this, it brings in the country managers into a corporate headquarter's function intermittently. It does not allow structure to overshadow functionality. The firm works smarter if it tends to be flat, does not allow the build up of bureaucracy around the corporate apex, and encourages cross-unit efforts.

A smart business enterprise is not only information savvy but is fully cognizant of the value of confidentiality in dealing with the competitive environment. Nature has given the gift of practising confidentiality only to human beings. The importance of maintaining confidentiality during the interactions with outsiders does not detract from the merit of being transparent or up-front in one's dealings. We live in a world where there are lurking forces out to misuse somebody else's private domain and make an intrusive peep into somebody's proprietary information. There are ways and means that your adversary can employ to penetrate into the protected sphere of your firm's activity. An awareness about this can be fostered through security orientation programmes conducted as part of the human resource training. A firm is not impeded by the threats from the rivals; it is in fact, empowered by the knowledge it comes to acquire about them.

A smart firm is led by people who know that a gap between idea and action can often be the principal cause of failure. A good strategy gets nowhere if it does not get communicated down the line for implementation. More organizations get hurt by the ill-effects of blocked communication lines than by the fallout of any honest mistakes. A fail-safe communication of ideas and directions within the organization is the cornerstone of the firm's operational success. The leadership of the enterprise must establish an organizational language in which the vision and the challenges facing the firm can be explained and understood by all without the risk of misinterpretation. A competent organization leadership is also aware that the senior echelons of management could unwittingly be 'holding on' to knowledge to retain an upper hand over others within the organization. They could be harbouring the notion that sharing knowledge is sharing power. Any such self-debilitating tendencies within the enterprise should be strongly curbed.

A firm should be convinced that strategizing in business is not a one-time event and it evolves with the firm's interplay with competitors and the competitive factors. New information or learning may compel a corrective action to remove a deficiency that had not been detected earlier or to utilize the discovery of a new source of competitive advantage. In the new dynamics of change, the firm's capacity to make course corrections has acquired added importance. Businesses today are on an evolutionary trajectory which means that there will always be something new to cope with. There may be a sudden setback but there is nothing like a permanent failure. New information and new permutations can once again create a helpful situation that has to be seized. A smart firm lives in the excitement of the showing it makes and looks upon a failure as just a contingency in which the effort made did not bring in the desired result.

A smart firm believes that anything that does not add value is waste. Before a company can improve its output, everyone who is a part of it has to really understand waste. Productivity is getting more done with the same or less. Corporate loyalty is emerging as a major reason why a member would produce the best results for his working time and also be on the look out for anything that reduces waste. Loyalty, however, is not built in a day. It is rooted in trust and you trust those whom you know well. The leaders of management must know the employees. The employees must know the managers and trust them. Once this happens, an aura of loyalty would run through the enterprise. Commitment is an important ingredient of loyalty. A loyal member sticks to the organization when the latter is in difficulty. He owns the challenge facing the company and thinks of contributing his mite to the responses of the enterprise to that challenge. This occurs in the firms which believe in nurtural and participative supervision and create a family feeling among the corporate employees. Smart management fosters the belief that in the security of the enterprise also lies the well being of the employees.

The business world is now realizing that corporate governance has no meaning unless there is a conscious adoption of ethical practices by the organization. Absence of a transparent internal code of business ethics may encourage wilful compromises, selfishness on the part of the executives, and a progressive dilution of the collective will of the enterprise to stem a rot. A string of financial scams affecting the corporate sector in India and abroad in the last few years have shown how a silent majority just watched the collapse of the organization because there were no defined codes of conduct to empower it against the few erring individuals who were visibly causing the wreck. An intelligent firm realizes that an ethical corporate working establishes its operational system on a stable footing and gives it an image that would deter individual misdemeanour.

Conclusion

Today, a sound strategy rests on the capacity of the business leader to integrate a multiplicity of determinants that set the competitive environment. A player with a superior sense of logic is likely to get an advantage over the rival because he is better placed to distinguish essentials from the non-essentials and get the benefit of a superior business analysis. A firm acts smart if it knows that in a competitive situation one can win not necessarily by 'waging a war' but by seeking mutual accommodation. A smart firm treats its work force as an assembly of individual performers and encourages it to produce new learning. It uses a person's particular talent or area of strength to make him or her produce more in less time. Such a firm realizes that a free flow of information through the company and easy communication among its organizational units will facilitate knowledge creation on one hand, and reduce the gap between instruction and action, on the other. Today, a company has to be sensitive to the customer's socio-cultural responses. It has to comprehensively understand that what does not add value is waste. Above all, a smart firm has the conviction that an ethical corporate working gives the enterprise a lasting stability.

References

1. *The Power of Simplicity*, Jack Trout, Tata McGraw Hill 1999.
2. Vilfredo Pareto : *Sociological Writings*, selected and introduced by SE Finer Pall Mall Press Ltd. London, 1966.
3. *The Strategy of Conflict* by Thomas C. Schelling, Harvard University.

19

Peak Performers

- **Security of information is best preserved when the firm establishes a management culture that understands security.**

The goal of any business enterprise is to convert investments into profit by keeping the combined cost of establishment, inventory, and operations below the money accruing on sales, by as far a margin as possible. It can normally do this by pursuing a two-fold strategy of handling the 'human' and 'process' fluctuations to keep the output stable and taking steps to ensure that the market demand for its product keeps up. The 'human' resource fluctuations are controlled by merit based recruitment, good in-house training, participative supervision, preservation of corporate loyalty, and incentives for good performance. The 'process' variations are stabilized by technological upkeep, inventory regulation, integral monitoring of the assembly line, swift delivery of the product, and contingency planning. As regards the market demand, the strategies have an entire range from building brand strength to handling customer relations. A firm that wants to perform well must ensure self-sufficiency of each of the sub-systems built around the various functional parameters defined above.

Pursuit of excellence brings competitive advantage. No firm can claim to have achieved perfection in all spheres of its functioning. Peak performers constantly strive to establish competitive bench-marking because they know that an early mover advantage that a firm might have had, could not be regarded as a permanent gain. A continual search for different and better ways of doing things within the overall strategic context is what will sustain the edge once acquired. The firms also have to steer clear of the well-known competitive blind spots like believing that what cannot be seen or assessed does not exist, that new and small competitors cannot pose a serious threat, or that a successful strategy yielding dividends in the present will hold good in the future as well.

Peak performers understand the factors that provide competitive advantage. They know that such an advantage grows fundamentally out of improvement, innovation and change. Innovation can manifest itself in a new product design, a new production process, or a new approach to marketing. Even a new way of training the personnel or reorganizing the structure of the firm may lead to better results. In other words, a company can hope to out-perform an equally renowned rival by re-conceiving its business's profit drivers. A deeper examination of what your customers care about in relation to your business or product can indicate the possibility of your meeting an additional concern of the customers so that the latter would be willing to pay more for getting what they value. There may be a new product-service mix waiting to be discovered during such an examination.

A high performer in business is willing to destroy its old advantages by creating new ones. In the 1990s, Nokia running businesses from power generation to production of tyres, cables and television, ran into shortage of funds. It decided to focus entirely on telecom and divested everything that was not telecom related. It got out of even some profitable businesses. It has since become the market leader in this line. The leadership of a peak-performing firm can define the focus of its business in simple terms. Ingar Kamprad of IKEA said 'the General who divides his resources will invariably be defeated' and he wanted his company to be known for concentrating on one thing at a time – in this case, it was making quality home furnishings available for the non-affluent.[1]

Today, the same information is available to everyone, thanks to the great democratization of knowledge sharing brought about by the IT revolution. If two firms have the same complete knowledge, their competitive advantage will lie in their ability to execute a futuristic plan based on that knowledge. If the same tool of technology is available to both, the one that has a management given to innovative thinking for producing new products and services, will score over the other. Smaller firms sometimes gain advantage over international rivals because they perceive a new basis of competing. Firms restructure or integrate their activities with suppliers and buyers to create a new value system. The leadership of an enterprise aspiring to become a peak performer must regard upgrading advantage as a normal part of its strategy. Peak performers seek out and act upon opportunities. In the business world, living on the edge and having the guts to seize a chance when you see it, is needed for gaining a competitive advantage.

In today's world, retaining the edge ultimately requires a global approach to strategy formulation. A global strategy involves coordinating and integrating activities on a world-wide basis for preserving a consistent brand reputation, serving international buyers, and gaining economies of scale. Simply operating internationally does not add up to a global strategy. Moreover, competing globally is not a substitute for improvements and innovation at home. In fact, a global approach is supposed to supplement home-based advantages.

Peak performers carry out a comprehensive competitor analysis workout as part of strategy formulation. They identify not only the other top performers in the industry but also the particular individuals that are gifted and dominant in those rival enterprises. It would be quite legitimate for a firm to try to bring them over to its side. If this is not feasible, then it might be just as well that the firm does not cross their path as a rival. A firm should always look across the entire commercial horizon for any emerging danger from the competition. A high profit company accumulating cash faster than it can invest in its own industry, is like a loose canon that could enter other businesses perceived to be making good profits and try to buy them out. This is a part of the scenario of corporate warfare being set by the global competition.

In the age of intelligence, there will be competition amongst the peak performers themselves. They have to find a new basis on which to create a competitive advantage. If two firms are performing excellently in the present, the only way one can gain over the other is by exploring the untested turf of the future. The most important advantage that such a firm can have is to acquire an early insight into the needs, environmental forces and trends that others have not noticed. To visualize an opportunity or to pick up early warning of an impending threat, and respond to it ahead of others is the key which can help a peak performer to get past an equally good rival. The firm should identify buyers with the most anticipatory needs and in fact investigate all emerging buyers or channels. It is the new types of buyers that often create the opportunity for shifts in the competitive position. Some regions lead in voicing concerns with social problems including environmental issues. Companies can get an early bird advantage by seeking these trend setters out because ultimately they set the direction in which all others would eventually move.

Peak performers seek out pressure and challenges instead of trying to avoid them. They like sophisticated buyers who are demanding and come up with difficult needs. Such buyers help the firm to upgrade performance and extend features and services. They serve as a laboratory for the firm's R & D. The firm likewise should opt for suppliers who have an insight that comes from the experience of international activities. A peak performing firm believes in training its employees on an ongoing basis, trying them out on new functions, and generally regarding them as a permanent work force on which pressures can be built for generating competitive advantage.

The peak performers know that what they need is 'intelligence innovators' and not mere knowledge workers because their staying on top will depend on the use of competitive intelligence for developing new lines of business and technology application. Business empires in times to come, will rise or fall depending on whether they have the foundation of 'intelligence' or not. This means that success in business would rest on the ability to either access intelligence directly or – and this is more likely–to have dependable instruments of business analysis to cull out that intelligence from the openly available information. A successful global player will have set apart human, financial, technological, infrastructural, and informational resources for competitive intelligence analysis. It would, of course have a system to consolidate in an ongoing manner, its own knowledge inventory rooted in the information existing within the company itself.

An illustrative application of analysis based competitive intelligence is the evaluation of the prospects of achieving a successful merger or acquisition. For such an analysis, the things to look for would include the desirability of the two entities sharing a vision and willing to play their complementary roles in it, short term gains for the employees of the acquired company or the merging firm, long term strategy needed for the united enterprise, similarity of cultures and the organizational chemistry, and the relevance of geographical proximity of the uniting organizations. The analysis may further get into the finer part of determining the segments on which the uniting entities will respectively focus on. It may become necessary even to assess who will be the competitors of the merged organization in the future and what will be the nature and strength of their challenge in the period ahead.

A peak performing firm adopts the strategy of maintaining a continuing relationship with centres of research and the sources of most talented people. The enterprise must identify the places where the best new knowledge relevant to that industry is being created. Further, incorporation of new thinking in the management process is often speeded up by the induction of some outsiders from other industries or from the company's own foreign subsidiaries. Finally, peak performers never give up their drive for relentless improvement because they know that firms which remain a stationary target are eventually overtaken by rivals. Advantage once gained is only sustained by discovering better or cheaper ways of doing things.

Peak performers understand the basic reality that today we live in a complex world where small differences can lead to vastly disparate results, where a simple cause and effect relationship does not work as what we see may be the outcome of a multiplicity of causes, and where change is the only constant. They know that the stability of their business depends, among other things, on the dynamics of their handling of the variables within their industry and in the general competitive environment outside. They visualize the firm as a living organism whose body parts – the sub-systems – all require the oxygen of information flow to keep up their energy levels. In a rapidly changing global market, dysfunction or ailment of any part or wing of the organization will produce consequences for the others. A peak performing firm never forgets that it is a human organization whose internal rhythm may be affected by human frailties. It is prepared to use flexibility for enhancing its resilience. For this, it ensures that the bureaucratic concept of compliance is replaced by a practice of thoughtful execution without fear of failure or reprimand.

Peak performers are strong in their pursuit of a dynamic business strategy designed to handle the challenge of change. Such a strategy is not reactive but pro-active since the peak performers like to lead the change. They know that there are no permanent friends or rivals in business. Microsoft's internet strategy began from a determined targeting of America Online but subsequently embraced a close long-range partnership with the latter. A high performing organization does not allow bureaucratization of its structure because this can come in the way of coordinating change successfully. The collapse of the Soviet Union's economic strategy is attributed to its overbearing and extremely rigid bureaucracy. Competitive advantage lies in the ability to have an early peep into the future but the firm's strategy should not be so obsessed with the future as to relax on the execution of its core competencies in the present. Strategy is all about knowing where the firm wants to go from where it stands and visualizing how that journey would be completed. Strategy means forward movement and a peak performer in business knows this.

Peak performers are ever willing to embrace change caused by the shifting market and the competitive terrain. While leading change, they maintain their vision so that the transformation efforts retain a sense of direction. Constant communication of the nature and purpose of these efforts to the employees down the line is extremely important. A classical intelligence organization is functionally and structurally flexible about making changes to deal with the changes in the threat scenario. A management practice that businesses can learn from the intelligence organization is to have built-in arrangements for a close monitoring of the progress of any transformation effort. An intelligence organization ends a project only if its utility disappears. A high performer always shows a co-relationship between his moves and the ground realities of their context.

Peak performers can sense that winning is a habit. They know that winning is hard work; it involves facing problems and solving them. For them a failure is just an interruption, a cross-roads not a cliff, or an effort that just did not bring in the right result. The psyche of a winner is to be ever prepared to put in that crucial extra effort which gives a momentum to the process of ensuring victory. Businesses that perform well have a built-in confidence in their capacity to deliver just as a classical intelligence organization is imbued with an innate determination to achieve its task.

Conclusion

A peak performing business stays with its edge by being in a constant pursuit of excellence and open to innovation and change. If two top firms are performing at par in the present, their competitive advantage will lie in their ability to produce new products and services or perceive a new basis of competing. A peak performer, today, has to compete globally and has to remember that operating internationally does not add up to a global strategy. It has to acquire an early insight into the needs, environmental forces, and trends that others have not noticed. It will always have a system for consolidating, in an ongoing manner, its knowledge inventory rooted in the tacit information that exists within the company itself. A peak performing firm maintains a continuing relationship with centres of research and the sources of most talented people. Such a firm tends to be flat discouraging any build-up of bureaucracy around its corporate apex. It knows that the stability of its business depends on the dynamics of its handling of variables within that industry and in the competitive environ outside. A peak performer leads change.

Reference

1. *The Complexity Advantage* by Susanne Kelly, Marry Ann Allison, McGrew Hill, 1999.

20

The Age of Intelligence

- **Fear of failure can cause cessation of learning.**

The knowledge era is seeing a rapid rise of the importance of ideas and strategies that can guide individuals and organizations into the future. It is the ability to perceive something located in a futuristic dimension, that will determine their competitive advantage. Today, information is universally shared as soon as it is created. Everyone therefore has access to the same open information. When two rivals have the same information resource, the one who will use it for the right decision first, would get the edge. Transforming the commonly shared information into intelligence or knowledge that yields an insight into the opportunities or threats lying ahead, is what will be of paramount importance. To be able to construct special meanings out of the available information and churn out readings that are exclusively your own, puts you in the lead. You have created competitive intelligence out of the information through analysis.

We are clearly at the threshold of the age of intelligence in which only intelligent organizations and enterprises converting knowledge into opportunities would survive. Such an enterprise needs to have its members equipped with this new-found awareness of what intelligence is.

It is less likely that you would have direct access to intelligence about your rival's thinking and moves. The human mind is however gifted with the ability not only to logically analyze the information that it comes across but also to anticipate what the others might be thinking in a given situation. This is 'lateral thinking' which makes it possible to foresee the moves of another player on your turf. It is synonymous with 'intelligence.' Lateral thinkers are at par with intelligence professionals. They are of an inventive frame of mind and are good detectives. They can travel up and down in the train of thought while pursuing a clue and are alive to the shifting probabilities in human responses. Anticipation or forward thinking is nothing but applied intelligence and it will be the hallmark of the Age of Intelligence that is closing upon us.

Complete intelligence is difficult to come by and the Age of Intelligence will create situations where you must be able to make decisions and act even with incomplete information. Moreover, ambiguity is something we will have to learn to live with. The action-taker may have to reckon with seemingly contradictory situations and be different from people who cannot deal with ambiguity.

A successful firm is aware of the importance of information of intelligence value that can be obtained through inter-action with the right people. In its essence, intelligence is all about knowing what certain individuals you are interested in, are thinking of doing. Skills of conversation and the art of interview are among the prize possessions of people who serve an intelligent business organization. Striking a friendly grid is a prerequisite for any meaningful exchange of views. Since every individual has some subjects he is easy with, the ability of the interviewer lies in making a smooth transit to a subject of the former's choice to create that grid. Use of social engineering techniques to lead the subject to make an unconscious disclosure of the information that he would not have normally parted with, is an acceptable part of 'intelligence' methodology. In the age of intelligence, successful organizations will give primacy to making their staff information savvy.

An intelligent enterprise is a huge training ground where there is constant grooming of the members to enable them to develop their human resource potential. The learning never ends because the challenge never ceases. The organization ensures that important lessons are drawn from everybody's experience. There are no text books to learn from and the organizational wisdom comes from the real-time operations. The corporate body replicates an important training concept of a classical intelligence organization – using specific experiences to formulate generic guidelines which, in turn, help to transpose a solution in a new moment of challenge. In the Age of Intelligence, no two business situations will exactly be the same ever and successful decision-making will rest primarily on the intelligence derived from case studies and from a competent analysis of the updated information available till then.

In the age of intelligence, innocence will be no excuse. Wisdom is intelligence used for a good cause but intelligence can also be misused for purposes of low cunning. An intelligent entity can detect the odour of craftiness emanating from the other party. It, however, does not turn away from trying to know the reality of an adverse situation or threat. Remember that ignoring the facts will not change them and that if you do not get the problem right you will not get the right solution. Competitiveness is fast becoming a source of the desire to reach the short-term objective regardless of the means. It is generating a belief that in this race there will be survival of the 'cleverest' rather than the 'fittest.' However, only those who act in wisdom by not sacrificing the long-term gain for a short-term advantage, will achieve the ultimate goal. People deliver the best results by doing the right things because crookedness always burdens the soul and hampers the output. Among the living beings, man alone lives consciously for a purpose and likes to have the feel of advancement on the path of virtue. An intelligent firm should watch out for anyone whose will to perform is only connected with his compensation package. Such a member is a potential target of the cunning adversary.

In business, like in any other sphere of human activity, goals are linked with visions and dreams. A dream can revolve round a mere wishful thinking but the vision is always the anchor of an achievable dream. The goal is the first milestone on the journey in the quest of that vision. This journey takes the firm from the present towards the future. In the age of intelligence, watching the flanks would be as important as remaining focused on the goal. The leadership of an 'intelligent' enterprise will be ready to handle the change of pace. The goal may move away or come closer as the journey runs into obstructions or hits a turf of extraordinary smoothness. Changes bring in an opportunity or an impediment; both have to be responded to competently and swiftly. The firm will need intelligence inputs for this. The age of intelligence is evolving out of the knowledge era. There is hope in this because the dynamics of evolutionary change always carry promises of new openings.

The age of intelligence however can setoff a trend that could, in turn, produce uncertain repercussions. The socio-political history of the world has witnessed from time to time, the rise of brotherhood of the strong against the relatively weak. A kinship of the successful is making its presence felt in the new knowledge economy. In the global competition, rivals are beginning to join hands to monopolize the market place. Pareto's Law that 'a few govern the many' had established the fact that it is the elite that always rule the large masses in all societies. This seems to have the potential of translating into the world economy as well in the sense that the alliance of the rich and the powerful could attempt to dominate the global scene.

A possible understanding between the political elites and the global players of business could start giving new meaning to sovereignty and this could promote a new form of hegemonism that the economically weaker nationalities will find so difficult to challenge. Movement of money through borderless markets, instant connectivity in the cyber space and a give-and-take amongst the ruling elite may increasingly come into play creating a disconnect between the rulers and the ruled in the less developed parts of the world. This may produce areas of instability on account of popular discontent and a further escalation of the asymmetric warfare in the form of endemic insurgencies and terrorism. State and non-State players may collude with each other to make matters worse. Hopefully there would be many leaders of business and politics who would like to take decisions that do the largest good to the largest numbers and inject sanity in international relations.

Intelligent nations would encourage public-private partnerships at home. Intelligent enterprises would also redefine their relationship with the State. Both would realise that there is no hope for development without business just as in the long-term, there is no business without development. Enlightened business interests will be 'the co-architects of development strategies' and join in public-private partnerships for 'building strong communities filled with prosperous citizens.'[1] The age of intelligence is already setting off this process.

Perhaps the most remarkable facet of the age of intelligence would be the increasing pressure for globalisation of intelligence itself. The pre-emptive attack on Iraq by the US-led coalition against the 'new terror' in 2003 raised the demand for a global scrutiny of the role of intelligence in determining the issues of war and peace. The independent commissions of inquiry subsequently appointed in the US and the UK, made some adverse comments on the quality of intelligence both in relation to 9/11 as well as the war on Iraq. Their findings were utilised for restructuring and upgrading the Intelligence set-up in the two countries. Their significance, however, lies in the fact that the intelligence base on which the action against Iraq was launched, was subjected to a public scan atleast partly in response to the opinion of the international community. The wide criticism of the war on Iraq reflected the concern of the world community that the US, as the only superpower in the world, might be pursuing a 'might is right' policy out of a desire to dominate the world economy.

Today when markets have no national boundaries, economic independence is becoming a major determinant of political sovereignty. In the age of intelligence a nation's strength will lie not merely in its military capability but also in its strength in other areas of strategic importance such as self-sufficiency in foodgrains, water resources, energy, educated citizenry, and a society free of internal conflicts. It is clear, therefore, that today strategic planning for development itself has become an intelligence-based endeavour. It needs a constant evaluation of all relevant information to uncover new opportunities and ways of doing things in a quicker and cost-effective manner. It calls for making use of technology and bench-marks available anywhere in the world outside. Competent governing of a nation is like running a huge enterprise on a note of success. It demands appropriate strategies to deal not only with geo-political adversaries but with the rivals in the global economy as well.

To sum up, the age of intelligence will be marked by the following seven characteristics: First, it will call for gathering and developing quality information rather than hoarding a vast quantity of information. Second, crucial business decisions will be based on intelligence and not on information that is available to everyone else. Third, the firms will have 'intelligence innovators' and not mere knowledge workers as their most valuable assets. This is because it will become crucially important to develop new lines of business and application of technology. Fourth, in the age of intelligence, truly competitive companies will become increasingly sophisticated in collecting information through the use of special skills of intelligence gathering. Fifth, analysis to convert information into intelligence will acquire primacy. There will be a renaissance of human intervention by way of analysis, in all aspects of strategy formulation. Sixth, business enterprises will be founded on intelligence. Intelligence will help the organisation to succeed not only when presented with opportunity but also in the face of obstacles or opposition. Lastly, winning in the age of intelligence will not mean that every body else loses. Your enemies may become your strongest allies. 'War rooms' will be replaced by 'Intelligence Innovation Labs.' There would be a wider acceptance of the view that a more ethical approach to business yields better results.

Conclusion

The knowledge era is paving the way for the arrival of the age of intelligence in which converting the commonly shared information into intelligence that gives an insight into the opportunities or threats lying ahead, will determine the competitive advantage. Only intelligent organizations transforming knowledge into opportunities by using anticipation or forward thinking, will survive in the new age. Legitimate use of intelligence methodology will become more common. In handling the challenge of change, intelligence will be the only means of knowing whether the changes are bringing in a new opening or indicating an impediment. The scene of 'corporate warfare' being set by the intense competition, is likely to throw up the Darwinian trend of a brotherhood of the strong trying to eliminate the relatively weak and monopolizing the marketplace. An understanding between the political elite and the global players of business, could promote a new form of hegemonism. Intelligence sharing could further strengthen this trend. In turn, there would be an increasing demand for a global scrutiny of the role of intelligence in determining the issues of war and peace. The pre-emptive invasion of Iraq by the US-led coalition in 2003 has brought this matter to the fore.

Reference

1. Rajat Gupta, Partner, Mckinsey & Company at the 60th UN General Assembly on Millennium Development Goals. September 15, 2005.

21

Intelligence Failure

- **Intelligence calls for a pro-active response from action takers.**

It is generally believed that there are more intelligence failures than successes. This perception arises primarily from the fact that any failure of intelligence elicits heavy public costs whereas the success is subsumed in the unseen continuity of the national security or the corporate progress as the case may be. Intelligence is not a commodity that can be ordered on payment; it is the natural outcome of an untiring and sincere effort to get at the bottom of what is thought to be there but is not visible. Intelligence is a security weapon because it helps a nation or an enterprise to protect itself against the covert threats from an adversary or a rival. Intelligence is also needed to fill in crucial gaps in the picture that an analysis of open information might be able to produce. An enemy may be known to be harbouring a plan to harm your country as there is enough information signalling his hostile intentions but the time frame of his intended assault can come only from hard intelligence. 9/11 signified a classical intelligence failure, both in terms of lack of information and an absence of pro-active analysis of whatever little had become known. The US-led pre-emptive war on Iraq in March 2003 was, on the other hand, based on intelligence that turned out to be unreliable and infact, contrived.

An understanding of the road map of intelligence is necessary to pin-point where exactly intelligence has failed in a particular case. Viewing it in a broad spectrum that is prone to changes, the world is full of friends and foes at any given point of time and the first requirement of intelligence is that there should be a regular information flow from the friendly turf as well as the unfriendly territory. This raises the basic problem of 'penetration' for creating sources of information in the inimical or rival establishment. With the advent of the new global terror arising from the developments in Afghanistan and Iraq following 9/11, the Western intelligence agencies have been sharply reminded of this fundamental weakness they had on the question of reaching out to the regions from where the new threat was originating.

MI6, Britain's overseas intelligence agency, has woken up to the need for having a greater mix of staff with a higher number of ethnic minorities to help infiltrate and combat terrorist networks linked to Al-Qaeda. The home page of the agency's first external website clearly states that the Secret Intelligence Service (SIS) – MI6's preferred name, 'provides the British government with a global covert capability to promote and defend the national security and economic well-being of the U.K.[1] This step has been taken to facilitate the process of recruitment from a wider base. A similar effort is being made by the CIA to cast its net far and wide for the positioning of its spies and spymasters in the light of its experience in Iraq. A primary cause of intelligence failure is the paucity of information channels or the failure of information production itself. As part of an ambitious strategy to rebuild US Human Intelligence after the debilitating lapses over Iraq and 9/11, the US has created a new agency called the National Clandestine Service or NCS which will operate out of the CIA under a director reporting to CIA Chief Porter Goss. With the new clandestine service based at his agency Goss will have a dual role as CIA Director and 'National Humint Manager.' Humint is bureaucratic parlance for human intelligence.[2]

Intelligence 'production' fails if a nation or an enterprise is not aware of what information it needs and where it can get this from? The leadership of a firm must have time to ponder over this matter. It should be mentally equipped to formulate the right questions that need to be answered before the firm's strategic decisions are taken. All nations have intelligence agencies to act as the eyes and ears of the government. In the competitive business environment of the kind produced by globalization, a firm must equip itself with the machinery that reaches out to information and analyzes it for producing competitive intelligence.

A basic ingredient of intelligence is its flawless credibility. Much bigger damage can be caused by unreliable information than by the sheer absence of intelligence altogether. In these days of 'dis-information' and 'double agents,' establishing the reliability of information before accepting it as intelligence has become very important. Evaluation of the source or the channel of information helps a great deal in this. A second hand information will particularly call for confirmation through a collateral route. The question of reliability of intelligence was raised by the Independent 9/11 Commission in the USA and also by the Commission in the UK that examined the basis of intelligence behind the Anglo-American war on Iraq. Intelligence failure results from lack of information and from information whose credibility is in doubt.

Intelligence, by definition, is information that is meant for action and since intelligence unravels a threat in a time frame, it is extremely important that intelligence is made available to the action takers without any loss of time. Speedy communication of intelligence is as important as the intelligence itself. It is not infrequent that delayed dissemination of intelligence, its dispatch to wrong quarters, or its distortion in transit comes in the way of a timely response. The Kargil Review Committee headed by Dr. K. Subrahmanyam examined in detail the intelligence inputs that were available before Pakistan's intrusion in Kargil in 1999 and revealed the systemic inadequacies that pervaded the then existing practices of communication and evaluation of intelligence. Intelligence from important sources did not reach the assessment making body at the national apex. The Brigade Intelligence Team of the 121 Infantry Brigade which was the first agency to detect the Pak intrusion on May 3, 1999 had been sending reports during 1998 on an ongoing increase in the appearances of militants and even Pak military personnel in civil dress but these never made it to what is now the National Security Council Secretariat. They were interpreted by the Brigade Headquarters in a piecemeal fashion as routine activity. The KRC listed out over 60 intelligence inputs furnished by the civil and military agencies through the second half of 1998 which did not all reach the Joint Intelligence Committee (JIC). If the system would have ensured examination at one place, of all these pieces of information representing the total intelligence available on what was happening on the LOC in Kargil sector, the analysts at the top might have noted the significance of the progression of information that was coming in and might have sounded the alarm bells much earlier than May 1999.[3] Kargil, therefore, represents a case of failure in terms of inadequacy of communication of available information.

Intelligence failure can be caused not merely by the failure of production and dissemination of information but also by the failure of analysis. The function of analysis is to put all pieces of information together and give it the meaning in terms of defining the character and timing of the threat. The Independent 9/11 Commission in the US commented on two major flaws of analysis that were behind the intelligence failure in regard to the terrorist attack on the WTC at New York. The biggest pitfall of intelligence analysis is for it to get influenced by the prejudices or bias of the policy makers. The diagnosis of the 9/11 Commission was that the analysts fell victim to 'group think' assumptions. They made analytical judgments 'not supported by the underlying intelligence.' According to psychologists, this happens when a group makes a decision 'based on the desire for unanimity rather than on the quality of the choice.'[4] The Commission made another remarkable point. It said that there was failure of 'imagination' on the part of analysts. In today's world, the analysts have to take the intelligence to the realm of 'anticipation.' The analyst cannot merely say what the picture is as indicated by the given facts but has to go into what can be 'forecast' beyond the picture that has become visible. In these days of paucity of intelligence, the increased importance of the study of modus operandi of terrorist groups for instance, can greatly help analytical deductions. Intelligence analysis function has generally become far more demanding intellectually.

If there is information of intelligence value and its analysis brings out a threat, then the most important thing is the response from those who are supposed to act on it in pursuance of the sovereign power of defending the nation, given to them. Failure of action results either from the lack of ability of the consumers to grasp the importance of intelligence or from a defective process of decision-making marked by turf divides and other flaws of leadership. Analyzing the character of the security failure in respect of 9/11, the Independent Commission in USA rightly put a share of blame on both intelligence producers and the consumers. The Commission ruled that even though there was not specific 'actionable' information about 9/11, the 'inconclusive warnings' should not have been disregarded. In this context, what happened to the famous August 6, 2001 Memo that the CIA director put before the Principals including the National Security Advisor for deliberations, provides a good case study. Captioned 'Bin Laden determined to strike inside the US,' it basically said that Al-Qaeda members had travelled to the US where a support structure was maintained by them. The Memo revealed enough for the security establishment to get going on a war-footing to unearth further leads. It should have led the Principals, particularly the National Security Advisor, to task both external and domestic intelligence and counter-intelligence agencies to work out the information further. Even if a specific prediction of 9/11 was not there, the August 6 Memo deserved a pro-active response from the leaders of the government. This did not happen. The Principals in this case took an arm-chair view and did not seem involved enough with the information made available to them. The case typically illustrates the familiar tendency of the consumers and action-takers to under estimate intelligence and adopt a laid-back attitude towards it. In Kargil there was a tardy response to the information that had first come in.

Nobody can ordinarily be permitted to sit on intelligence that has been furnished by the national intelligence organisation. The intelligence agency puts its entire reputation at stake when it releases the information for use by the decision-makers. The formidable accountability that goes with ordering a response, sometimes prompts the action takers to buy time by raising diversionary questions of veracity or adequacy of information. The principle that applies here is that if while executing the response a flaw in intelligence is detected, then the agency would be held answerable in a big way. Those who act on information cannot encroach on the turf of the information producers, by seeking to examine the sources of information unless of course there are some good reasons for questioning the credibility of the information at any stage.

In the Indian context, I recall how at one point of time in 1995, I took strong exception to the inordinate delay on the part of the armed forces in acting on a piece of concrete intelligence furnished by the Intelligence Bureau in connection with the case of the Harkat-ul-Ansar sponsored kidnapping of Western tourists in Kashmir Valley. When the matter was looked into, on my insistence, it was found that the 'turn around' period of the nearest armed unit was much too long. Corrective measures were then taken to modify the deployment.[5]

In today's fast moving world, the gap between information and action is getting reduced. The US had to face this challenge in conducting its war on terror. The CIA has 600-700 covert operators who are like combatants. They were used on the Afghan front. In November 2001, the US President issued the order committing the Armed Forces to an unconventional warfare that was to be fought through 'covert operations.' In counter-terrorism operations, there is a constant inflow of tactical intelligence which has to be acted upon by the forces available in close proximity. We know from our own experience that our paramilitary forces like the BSF, while conducting counter-insurgency operations, generate a lot of field intelligence. In US, the Pentagon waged the unconventional warfare through the military's Special Operations Command (SOCOM) which has roughly 10,000 combatants. What is more, the Pentagon created a new post of Under Secretary of Defence for Intelligence to channelize the flow of intelligence for action. A situation can develop sometimes when the intelligence personnel may have to become part of the action unit – operationally, though not organizationally. The security system must rise above turf conflicts to bring this about.

Perhaps the most important precept highlighted by the Independent 9/11 Commission in the US was that national security does not admit of a divided turf. The Commission revealed how there was a complete compartmentalization between the external dimensions of security and the so-called internal or domestic threats. Deposing before the Commission, Dr. Condoleezza Rice, the then National Security Advisor, took the defence that Al-Qaeda was a foreign policy agenda thereby raising the question whether the National Security Advisor was responsible for only half of the national security. 9/11 was an attack on the internal security of the US but its origins lay outside the country. India also is typically a country where the external dimensions of security and the internal threats have a cause and effect relationship. A security system not integrating the two does not do justice to its responsibility. The US Commission said it all in one sentence – 'America's homeland defenders faced outwards.' The report revealed an interesting fact that legal and structural impediments apparently affected intelligence sharing between the CIA and the premier counter-intelligent agency in the US, the FBI. It is a matter of great satisfaction that in India any such disabilities do not exist. Both external and internal intelligence agencies report to the National Security Advisor here.

A security failure can thus be caused by the failure of coordination among various agencies generating intelligence and the wings of the government responsible for taking action on the intelligence provided. A path-breaking recommendation made by the 9/11 Commission that has already been implemented in the US is that a new National Director of Intelligence (NDI) should take over from the Director CIA the function of coordinating the intelligence agencies. This provides for an intelligence oversight at the national apex. Further, the US has established a National Counter-Terrorism Centre (NCTC) connected to a dozen US agencies including the CIA and the FBI and feeding information online to 4000 counter-terrorism experts across the government.[6] Its Chief Redd is the President's top advisor on terrorism but he is also answerable to National Intelligence Director John Negroponto.

Security failure therefore can be caused by the failure of intelligence production, communication or analysis, lack of action, or the absence of systemic coordination. An integral security system anywhere, should have an authority like the NDI to preside over a joint apex at the national level, of which the heads of all the existing national intelligence agencies are a part. The National Security Council of India will be served better by an intelligence infrastructure functionally integrated at the top through the institution of a participatory National Intelligence Board.

Just as failure of intelligence can jeopardize national security, lack of competitive intelligence can result in a grave setback to a business enterprise. If a firm fails to reach out to information that indicates an opportunity or misses out on information that carries signals of an impending threat, it can lose in competition. Businesses face danger from adversaries who could be initiating covert moves against them to subvert their image and product strength, entice away their key functionaries and even steal their trade secrets. Rivals may form an alliance to run down a targeted player. Even techniques of 'misinformation' and 'disinformation' are used to create changes in the market. A new threat has arisen in the era of IT, of clandestine attacks on the core information systems. In order to damage national security the enemy today is tempted to destroy the information systems of the core sectors of the economy and business services. The forces behind the global terror are reportedly engaged in planning such strikes. It is said that in China, the People's Liberation Army (PLA) is developing a line of warfare in which the power of nuclear weapons will be countered in the cyber space through a recourse to the destruction of the enemy's information system serving the war machine. Today, the security of an enterprise also means the security of its information system and its proprietary content.

Conclusion

It is not generally understood that a security failure may result not only from a failure of information production itself but may be the outcome of the failure of those who are responsible for assessing and acting on the intelligence provided. The function of analysis in terms of defining the character and timing of the threat is extremely important. In today's world, the analysts have to use intelligence for entering into the realm of anticipation and forecasting beyond the visible picture that has been drawn by the information at hand. Since complete intelligence is difficult to come by, there should be a pro-active response to whatever has been revealed. For a business enterprise also, it is a matter of survival for it to protect itself against the covert threats from an adversary or a rival. If a firm fails to reach out to information that indicates an opportunity or if it misses out on information that carries signals of an impending threat, it can lose in competition.

References

1. *Hindustan Times*, New Delhi, October 14, 2005.
2. *The Times of India*, New Delhi, October 15, 2005.
3. *Intelligence, a Security Weapon* by D.C. Pathak, Manas Publications, Delhi, 2003.
4. *New Politics of Intelligence* by Richard Betts, Foreign Affairs, June 2004.
5. *'Intelligence—a Security Weapon'* by D.C. Pathak, Manas Publications, Delhi, 2003.
6. *Hindustan Times*, New Delhi, 'US Claims progress in terror fight', October 14, 2005.

22

Media and Intelligence

- **All intelligence is information but all information is not intelligence.**

There are many commonalties between the profession of intelligence and a career in journalism. First of all, both handle information about human thinking and activity. Intelligence is about man-made disasters; it does not forecast an earthquake for instance, and if media covers the event, it does so primarily because of the impact that the seismic phenomenon has on human life. Intelligence operators and journalists are all the time exploring a human situation and tracking a human target. Media wants to know all about the Page-3 crowd; intelligence is keen to ascertain what the ruling elite of a hostile country is upto. It is ultimately the coverage of individuals that matters for both. In intelligence it is the mind that rules the game. Journalism however can be a calling of the heart as well as the mind. This is how media can bring out the plight of the common man and give his story the social relevance of a kind that is designed to shake the conscience of the world.

The second link that puts media and intelligence on the same side of the fence is the commitment they have towards the credibility of the information that they put into use. Unverified information can lead to intelligence failure with all its disastrous consequences. A media report lacking in credibility also causes serious damage both to the individual reporter as well as the organization that he or she represents. In intelligence, the standards for establishing reliability of the information are extremely rigorous because the cost of failure can be very high. Good journalism also rests on the accuracy of information. Journalists have an advantage that they report on what they see or hear themselves. This is particularly true of the electronic media with its capacity to provide live visuals and sound bytes. It is an accepted norm that whenever media unravels a scandal, it would have in its possession some solid evidence like a document to base it on.

Thirdly, information used by intelligence and the media, generally speaking, has some shade of confidentiality about it. Intelligence is information handled with complete secrecy for the reason that it gives the possessor an advantage over the enemy. Media keeps information under wraps to convert it into a 'breaking news' or an 'expose' and get the better of the rivals. In both media and intelligence, information is transmitted with great speed.

Fourthly, a competent analysis of facts is a common skill needed for success in the career of both intelligence and journalism. The quality of news analysis determines its value for the readers. Analysis creates space for competitors in the media. In intelligence however, the precepts of good analysis are so rigorously defined that it does not permit ambiguity of interpretation at all. This is because good intelligence is also to indicate what should be the most appropriate course of response to the information provided.

Finally, journalism relies on many skills of gathering and collating information that are so special to an intelligence organization. In both journalism and intelligence, a lot of useful information is taken from the 'shelves' or obtained from 'open' sources. Investigative journalism attempts to garner valuable facts through confidential channels. Journalists know the importance of carefully cultivated contacts. Secretly conducted inquiries and a discreet watch carried out within permitted legal parameters are also made use of. Interviews and interactions during social and business get-togethers are also put to good use by the young journalists who are adept at using 'cover' while pursuing their mission. Today, a successful journalist has an intelligence orientation.

Successful journalists and intelligence operators have the traits of an information savvy person. Such a person tends to read a lot, has an unsatiable curiosity and takes a healthy interest in human psychology and behaviour. He does not accept gossip, preferring an authoritative opinion instead and has the ability to distinguish the more significant from what is of lesser importance. He is logical when pursuing information and is able to think of the what why and where of any quest for information.

The basic differences between the professions of intelligence and journalism, however, need to be understood also. The media informs the public about the affairs of the State. Intelligence informs the State about the domestic and external situation. An avowed objective of the media is to protect the citizen from the 'wrong doings' of a government. Intelligence concerns itself with protecting the State from its enemies. Good journalism invariably helps intelligence and in turn, intelligence should also help journalists in appropriate situations. An intrinsic conflict, however, runs through the intelligence-media interface whenever investigative journalism starts probing into the operational methodology of the intelligence organization or seeking to convert what lies in the domain of secrecy into news. Sometimes, in the scheme of the media, the concern for the security of the State recedes into the background. Since media informs and also entertains, the 'fun' of unveiling secrets of individuals, organizations and the State only for generating the reader's interest, might motivate the journalist in individual cases.

In these times, the national intelligence organization cannot remain completely cut off from public view and cannot exist in total obscurity. The details of the operational work of the intelligence agencies must remain a secret but the public should be given some idea of the threats that jeopardize national security as also the broad directions in which the national security strategy was being pursued. The people should also know the highlights of the tangible results achieved in this regard. People in India are very sensitive to national security issues. The area of confidentiality that the State must have cannot be questioned and the limits of the right to information in the sphere of national security must be clearly defined. It should not, however, be difficult to give to the media what is needed for retaining confidence in national security and fostering public education. Media should also understand that there is no such thing as a 'selective leak.' Anything disclosed in confidence to a journalist would, in effect, be no different from what would have been consciously made public by the intelligence organization. Confidentiality is never a halfway house.[1] Media, all the same, is an important instrument for bringing the strategies of the government into the domain of public awareness. This is a feature of a democratically strong society.

Information relevant to national security, comes today from sources open to a far greater degree than was possible before the advent of the information age. This does not detract from the importance of intelligence that is always at the core of all threat assessments. However, in developed societies, the media, particularly investigative journalism, works to unearth whatever it thinks is against national interest and this places it on the right side of the security and intelligence setup of the country. If the media analysts draw up a projection on the security related facts, making sure that information used by them is reliable and if their analysis is not influenced or motivated by the desire to hog personal limelight, the results produced would complement the effort of the national security set-up.

A helpful relationship between the media and the security set-up is impeded by the contradiction that often surfaces on the issue of confidentiality and by the general reluctance that the secret agencies of the government develop about a two way exchange of information with the journalists. A healthy equation between a confident security set-up and a responsible media, however, is something that is both desirable and achievable. In western democracies as also in India, veteran journalists commanding national respect for their knowledge and insight are looked upon as a credible think-tank outside the government and their strategic projections always receive the attention of the policy makers. On the other hand, the reputed strategic analysts of the government often continue expressing their thoughts through the media even after they cease to hold the office of the State. Dr. K. Subrahmanyam, the noted defence analyst of India, is a good symbol of this convergence of media and the security set-up of the nation as far as the role of enhancing the awareness of strategic issues is concerned.

Conclusion:

Both intelligence and media men handle human activity and thinking, stand committed to the information they put out, and have a good understanding of what confidentiality means. They are geared to communicating information with speed. Investigative journalism utilizes many of the tools of intelligence-gathering, within the permitted legal parameters. Carefully cultivated contacts, secret inquiries, and interviews with or without the use of a 'cover' are the important techniques practiced by journalists. Successful journalists and intelligence operators are information savvy, curious to an unsatiable degree, and logical when pursuing information. With news analysis emerging as a strong point of journalism, media men can acquire a competitive advantage on the strength of how good they are in the classical skills required for competent assessment making. The role of media and intelligence is, broadly speaking, mutually complementary except in situations where investigative journalism starts probing into the operational methodology of the national intelligence organizations or begins to convert what lies in the domain of secrecy, into news. Both, however, have a congruence in the area of enhancing the national awareness on strategic issues.

Reference

1. '*Intelligence : A Security Weapon*', by D.C. Pathak, Manas Publications, Delhi, 2003.

23

Role of Business Schools

- **An intelligent enterprise has managers who discover what is unique about each person and then capitalize on it.**

It is ironical that the business schools, particularly in India, have not adequately imbibed the paradigm shifts that have been brought into play by the IT revolution across the entire spectrum of market analysis, ways and means of conducting business, and the basis of competition itself. The content of teaching and the pattern of thinking are still somewhat traditional. Importance of information-based decision-making, concept of intelligence, study of competitive environment, knowledge creation and information security does not specifically figure in the business management courses. No wonder many corporates are finding the new graduates of business schools too much glued to the textbook to easily settle down to the hands-on calls. They are not adequately geared to the new requirements of prompt communications and quick analysis. In many cases, these new entrants could even find this demand running against the notions of comfort of becoming the part of a settled corporate bureaucracy that they might have brought with them.

Today, a little neglect of supervision can cause a big derailment of the process of implementation. Delay in appreciating the value of information received can deprive the enterprise of an opportunity or expose it to an avoidable setback. If vertical interaction is impeded by bureaucratization, it can cause havoc in a situation where business is conducted with incredible speed. Even the attributes of a business leader have become more demanding and nuanced in the era of globalization.

Most business schools have not even attempted to add short modules of teaching on these subjects to their mainstream courses on business management. Competitive intelligence has created new concepts in human resource development, corporate loyalty, inventory control, value addition, brand strength, knowledge building, and 'due diligence.' Indian business is not corporatized enough with the result that not many case studies are available in the area of application of intelligence by the firms here. However, on the global scene, there is plenty to draw from, for the purposes of enriching the teaching on the impact of information and intelligence on business.

There are seven distinct chapters outlined below that deserve to be incorporated in some form in all management courses. First is the understanding of information and intelligence, the importance of being well informed and the imperatives that make timely and reliable information the basis of personal and professional success in this age of knowledge. There is a paradigm shift in what makes for success in business in a situation where your rival may not be around the corner but may be operating from any part of the globe.

Second is about the ways and means of accessing information that is internally available and acquiring knowledge of the external environ that shapes the prospects of business, particularly when new markets are being explored. There are multiple determinants of the information need in the age of globalization and a firm cannot do without information savvy executives in these times.

Thirdly, the business management must focus on the new criteria of the decision-making set by the information age and the requisites of leadership in business which are shifting from the attributes of personal charisma to the skills of acquiring a knowledge-based insight into the shape of things to come. Leadership is largely an ability to avail of the opportunity that is seen on the horizon, ahead of the competitors.

Fourthly, the success of a business decision more often than not, now depends on the analysis of the multiplicity of factors that would determine the prospects of the firm in the future. Even where comprehensive information is available, translating it into an instrument of action requires its collation and assessment for producing intelligence. The course of action will be determined by the business leader but he or she has to be in full awareness of this intelligence about the market and the forces playing out there.

Fifthly, a firm that can stand in competition is one that builds its personnel as knowledge workers who can generate new information while at work and help to put this information to use for innovative purposes and for value addition. Human

Resource Development has new tasks cut out for it – the chief of these being the responsibility for shifting management from the traditional bureaucratic approaches to a path of synchronization by emphasizing participative supervision, vertical interaction and pooling of knowledge for the organization.

Sixth is the rise of global managers who can work in markets across geographical frontiers and who can understand and respond to the politico-legal and cultural imperatives of the new regions. These managers are leaders in their own right who can, within the organizational code of conduct, exercise their legitimate discretion to the best advantage of the firm.

Last but not the least, firms are going to need arrangements to protect themselves from the invisible threats of the enemies and rivals outside as much as from the internal malcontents who may be misusing their authorized 'office' for personal gains at the cost of the enterprise. All this involves safeguarding of protected information, insulating the personnel from the prying attempts of the adversary, and keeping up security and vigilance awareness of the workers and managers. This is a new set of emerging responsibilities that can be discharged only on the authority of the top leadership of the firm. The business management schools are not sensitizing their students on this beyond perhaps introducing them to some conceptual treatment of corporate governance.

Conclusion

Business schools seem to have lagged behind in responding to the age of knowledge as they have not specifically incorporated education on information and information handling, in their management programmes. Importance of information-based decision-making, concept of intelligence, study of the competitive environment, knowledge creation, and information security are some of the vital subjects that have to be dealt with to equip the business school graduates with necessary preparedness that they would need for handling corporate responsibilities. Competitive intelligence has thrown up new concepts in human resource development, corporate loyalty, and value addition and business schools would do well to suitably enrich their main-stream courses by introducing instructions modules pertaining to the impact of information and intelligence on business.

Index